Mystery Sneaker

THEODORE CLYMER
RICHARD L. VENEZKY

Consultants
CLAIRE HENRY
DALE D. JOHNSON
HUGHES MOIR
P. DAVID PEARSON
PHYLLIS WEAVER

Ginn and Company

Acknowledgments: Grateful acknowledgment is made to the following publishers, authors, and agents for permission to use and adapt copyrighted material:

Atheneum Publishers, Inc., for "Our World Is Earth," adapted from *Our World Is Earth* by Sylvia Engdahl. Copyright © 1979 by Sylvia Engdahl. Reprinted by permission of Atheneum Publishers. Also for "Flashlight" from *Flashlight and Other Poems* by Judith Thurman. Copyright © 1976 by Judith Thurman. Reprinted by permission of the publisher.

Crown Publishers, Inc., for the adaptation of "Animal Fact/Animal Fable" by Seymour Simon. Reprinted from *Animal Fact/Animal Fable* by Seymour Simon, illustrated by Diane de Groat. Text copyright © 1979 by Seymour Simon. Illustrations copyright © 1979 by Diane de Groat. By permission of Crown Publishers, Inc.

Doubleday & Company, Inc., for "Amelia's Flying Machine," adapted excerpts from *Amelia's Flying Machine* by Barbara Hazen. Text copyright © 1977 by Barbara Shook Hazen. Reprinted by permission of Doubleday & Company, Inc.

Elsevier-Dutton Publishing Co., Inc., for "Winnie-the-Pooh," with selected illustrations, and for the portion of the Table of Contents on page 221, all from *Winnie-the-Pooh* by A. A. Milne. Copyright © 1926 by E. P. Dutton & Co., Inc. Renewal, 1954, by A. A. Milne. Reprinted by permission of the publisher, E. P. Dutton.

Harcourt Brace Jovanovich, Inc., for "My Friend Charlie" by James Flora. Abridged and adapted from *My Friend Charlie,* © 1964 by James Flora. Reprinted by permission of Harcourt Brace Jovanovich, Inc. Also for the poem "Primer Lesson" from *Slabs of the Sunburnt West* by Carl Sandburg, copyright 1922 by Harcourt Brace Jovanovich, Inc.; copyright 1950 by Carl Sandburg. Reprinted by permission of the publisher.

Harper & Row, Publishers, Inc., for "The Moon Singer," which is an adaptation of the complete text of *The Moon Singer* by Clyde Robert Bulla. Copyright © 1969 by Clyde Robert Bulla. By permission of Thomas Y. Crowell, Publishers. Also for "The Secret Three," adapted text of pages 7–46 from *The Secret Three* by Mildred Myrick. Text Copyright © 1963 by Mildred Myrick. An *I Can Read* Book. By permission of Harper & Row, Publishers, Inc., and of the publisher in the United Kingdom and British Commonwealth, World's Work Ltd. Also for the text of Chapter 15, "The Footbridge", and the excerpt on page 207 from the Table of Contents of *On the Banks of Plum Creek* by Laura Ingalls Wilder. Copyright, © 1937, as to text, by Harper & Row, Publishers, Inc. Renewed 1965 by Roger L. MacBride. By permission of Harper & Row, Publishers, Inc. Also for the text of "Change" from *River Winding:* Poems by Charlotte Zolotow. By permission of Thomas Y. Crowell, Publishers, and of the publisher in the United Kingdom and British Commonwealth, World's Work Ltd.

Houghton Mifflin Company for "All About Friends," adapted from *What Every Kid Should Know* by Jonah Kalb and David Viscott, M.D. Copyright © 1974, 1976 by Sensitivity Games, Inc. Reprinted by permission of the publisher, Houghton Mifflin Company. Also for "Sending Messages," adapted from *Sending Messages* by John Warren Stewig. Copyright © 1978 by John Warren Stewig. Reprinted by permission of the publisher, Houghton Mifflin Company. Also for the poem "Why the Sky Is Blue" from *Fast and Slow* by John Ciardi. Copyright © 1975 by. John Ciardi. Reprinted by permission of the publisher, Houghton Mifflin Company.

G. P. Putnam's Sons for "The Mixed-Up Mystery Smell," Parts 1 and 2, and for "Mrs. Birdie's Bread," all by Eleanor Coerr. Adapted by permission of G. P. Putnam's Sons from *The Mixed-Up Mystery Smell* by Eleanor Coerr. Copyright © 1976 by Eleanor Coerr.

Random House, Inc., for "The Friendly Dolphins" by Patricia Lauber. Adapted by permission of Random House, Inc. from *The Friendly Dolphins,* by Patricia Lauber. Copyright © 1963 by Patricia Lauber. Also for "The Case of the Missing Homework" by Lilian Moore. Adapted by permission of Random House, Inc. from *Everything Happens to Stuey,* by Lilian Moore. Copyright © 1960 by Lilian Moore. Also for "The Sack of Diamonds" by Helen Olson. Adapted by permission of Random House, Inc. from *Stupid Peter and Other Stories,* by Helen Kronberg Olson. Copyright © 1970 by Helen Kronberg Olson.

Charles Scribner's Sons for "Robin and the Sled Dog Race," adapted from *Robbie and the Sled Dog Race* by Sara & Fred Machetanz. Text copyright © 1964 by Sara Machetanz. Reprinted by permission of Charles Scribner's Sons.

Franklin Watts, Inc., for "Crafty Cardboard Houses," adapted from *Games for a Rainy Day* by Maurice Pipard. Copyright 1975. Used by permission of Franklin Watts, Inc.

Associated Book Publishers Ltd, London, for "The Footbridge" and for the portion of the Table of Contents on page 207, both from *On the Banks of Plum Creek* by Laura Ingalls Wilder. Published by Methuen Children's Books Ltd. Reprinted by permission.

Dodd, Mead & Company, Inc., for "I Meant to Do My Work Today" by Richard LeGallienne. Reprinted
(Continued on page 318)

2

Contents

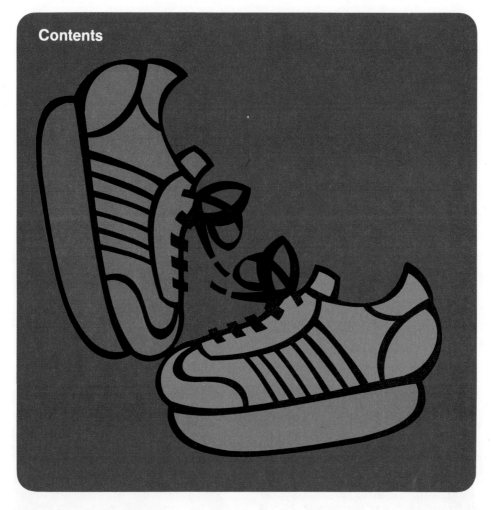

Have you ever felt happy because you had a really good friend? Someone who shares ideas with you, who laughs and cries with you, is a really good friend. Friendship can be wonderful!

The friendly people in this unit want to share some thoughts with you. Kate is involved in a mixed-up mystery. Something's in the air, and she can't even see it! Then Robin and her sled dogs want you to join them for an exciting race. It's so fast that it might lift you off your chair. Hold on! You also are invited to the sea. Some friendly dolphins want to chat.

Smile if you're ready to go side by side with the friends you are going to meet here. Get set! Go!

Side by Side

José and Charlie are a good team. They're getting
ready to visit the moon. So hurry! There's just
enough time to read about Charlie before lift-off.

My Friend Charlie

James Flora

Why I Like Charlie

My friend Charlie is a really good old friend. I couldn't like him any better than I do, even if he owned a pony.

There are lots of reasons I like Charlie. Here are some:

1. He gives me half of whatever he is eating.
2. Sometimes he lets me be the pitcher in the ball game, even though he owns the ball.
3. Charlie never laughs at my nose.

11

4. Sometimes when I am about to be eaten by dragons, Charlie saves me.
5. Once when I cut my hand, Charlie cried, too.

Another good reason is that Charlie can think of lots of good things to do. Let me tell you about some of them.

Charlie Saves a Cat

Cats like to climb up trees. They really hate to climb down. Some cats will sit up in a tree all day. They'll cry until someone comes to help them down. My friend Charlie always helps cats.

One day Charlie heard a "meow" up in a tree. That was the day he thought of a new way to get cats out of trees.

He went home and got a pail and a rope and a fish. He put the fish in the pail. Then he tied one end of the rope to the handle. He threw the other end of the rope over a branch up above the cat and pulled the pail up.

The cat smelled the fish and jumped into the pail. Then Charlie brought the pail down.

That cat had an elevator ride and a fish all at the same time. The cat liked it. Now it won't leave Charlie. The cat follows him everywhere. Charlie says it just wants more fish. But I think the cat really likes Charlie, just as I do.

Charlie Gets a Letter from the Moon

"I got a letter from the moon today," Charlie said. "Do you want to know what it says?"

"Sure," I said. "I never heard from the moon in my whole life."

"It says, 'Dear Charlie: I saw you the other night when you stayed up until ten-thirty playing hide-and-seek. That is too late, and your mother was worried. I hope you won't do that again.

'And why do you keep telling people that I am made of green cheese when you know very well that I'm made of rocks? Please tell the truth about me.

'Thanks for sending me all the peanut butter and jelly sandwiches last week. They were very good. I don't get much good food up here except when some kind friend remembers to send me some.

'Can you come up here for a visit next week? It

would be nice to have you. Bring your pajamas, and
you can bring your friend José if you like.

    'Best wishes,

        your friend, The Moon

'P.S. Please bring some new flashlight batteries
when you come. I think mine are wearing out. I
don't seem to shine as brightly as I did last year.' "

    "That's goofy," I said. "How can you go to the
moon? How can the moon eat peanut butter and
jelly sandwiches? And you know very well it
doesn't need batteries to shine. Where did you get
that goofy letter, Charlie?"

"I made it up," said Charlie. "I always wanted a letter from the moon, but I never got one until today. I think I'll go. Do you want to go along?"

We went and had a wonderful time. Just make-believe, of course.

Charlie Borrows My Dream

"I had a good dream last night," I told Charlie. "I dreamed that I had a bike that could go anywhere. I rode it right up one side of a tree and down the other. I rode it up and down all the houses on the way to school. When I got to school, I rode all over the room and sideways across the board. Our teacher was surprised."

"Say! That's a great dream," Charlie said. "Let me borrow that dream tonight. Will you? I'll let you dream my trip-to-the-moon dream. It's a good one, too."

17

"Sure, Charlie," I said. "You can borrow it tonight."

The next day Charlie said, "I sure do like that old bike dream of yours. I'm going to keep it a few more nights and add some nice parts to it."

Charlie dreamed my dream for a whole week. When he gave it back, it was much better. It had new parts in it. I ride the bike over mountains and tugboats. I ride it under the sea and over whales and right into the White House. Then the President says to me, "You are the very best bike rider in the whole country!" He shakes my hand and gives me a prize.

18

You can always tell when somebody is your friend. A friend sometimes borrows a dream. A friend takes good care of the dream. A friend fixes up the dream and gives it back better than ever!

Focus

1. Give three reasons Charlie was a good friend.
2. Charlie said the cat followed him because it wanted more fish. What was the other reason José gave for the cat's following Charlie?
3. Tell three things the Moon asked Charlie to bring on his visit.
4. Name one thing Charlie added to his friend's bike dream.

19

Down-to-earth talk about making and being a friend can give you some good ideas. Do you have any friendly advice to share?

All about Friends

Jonah Kalb and David Viscott

What Is a Friend

A friend is a person who likes some of the same things you like.

A friend is a person who trusts you and understands you. A friend likes you the way you are.

A friend is a person who shares some of the things you think are important.

A true friend already understands how you feel about things without having to be told. Friends understand how bad you feel because they hurt the same way.

Friends don't expect you to be perfect. You do the same for them.

How to Make Friends

Let's say you just moved to a new town. You don't know anyone. The best way to make friends is to do what you used to do. If you liked stamps in your old town, join a stamp club. If you liked sports in the old town, try out for some teams. If you were a singer, join a chorus. In that way, you will find people who like the things you do. You'll have a good time. It is easier to find friends when you're already having a good time.

Be Yourself

Being yourself is a good idea. You will make friends and keep them as well. Friends must be honest. You wouldn't want to make friends with somebody because you pretended to be someone you really weren't. You want friends to like you the way you really are. You are not perfect. Nobody is perfect.

Be a Friend

To make a friend, you have to be a friend. Be somebody that another person would like to have for a friend.

Focus

1. Name three things from the text that would end this sentence: A friend is somebody who. . . .
2. What are two ways to make friends in a new town?
3. Why should you be yourself when you want to find friends?

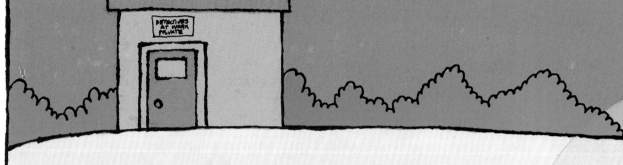

Kate, Marsha, and Nobby don't see anything in the air. And that's the problem. It's a real mixed-up mystery. Be a friend and help them look.

The Mixed-Up Mystery Smell, Part 1

Eleanor Coerr

Kate ran across the yard to the clubhouse. She was carrying a box. A sign over the clubhouse door said: Detectives at work. Private.

Kate pushed the clubhouse door open. "Look what I have!" she yelled.

Her friend Marsha was talking to Nobby.

"Tell us later," Marsha said. "We're busy thinking of a mystery to solve."

"But I have a mystery," Kate said. "It's here in this box."

"Okay, open it," Marsha told her.

Kate opened the box slowly.

Marsha looked inside. "There's nothing here," she said.

Nobby looked with his magnifying glass. "I can't see anything either," he said.

25

"There is so something inside," Kate said. "It's a mystery smell." She stuck her nose inside the box and sniffed hard. Then she looked with the magnifying glass. Marsha and Nobby sniffed, too.

"I don't smell anything," Marsha said.

"Neither do I," said Nobby.

"I've lost it!" Kate cried.

"Never mind," Marsha said. "Tell us about it."

"You know that empty old house on Grizzly Hill?" Kate asked.

"The one that's haunted?" Nobby asked.

"That's it," Kate said. "Now lights are on in the house, and there's a funny smell all around it."

Marsha laughed. "Maybe a wizard is in the haunted house making a brew of toads' ears and hairy spiders and crawly things."

Kate shivered. "It couldn't be that because it's not a bad smell. It's a kind of mystery smell."

"Whoever heard of a mystery smell?" Marsha said.

"If you don't believe me," Kate said, "go and sniff for yourself."

"We don't have any other mysteries today. Kate, take us to the smell."

Nobby put his detective notebook, pencil, and magnifying glass in a bag. Kate led the way. They stopped in front of an old brown tumbled-down house. The wind rustled dry leaves in the yard. The house looked empty and scary. A strange smell was all around. Kate sniffed.

"Here it is!" she yelled. "Can you smell it?"

Nobby took a long sniff. "That's interesting," he said. "There is a smell. It makes me hungry." He scribbled with his pencil in the notebook.

Marsha sniffed. "You're right, Kate. You always did have the best nose in the club." Kate rubbed her nose proudly.

"Well, we've got to solve this mystery," Marsha said. "Let's sniff and think."

They all sat down.

Soon Kate got tired of sniffing and thinking. "My nose won't work anymore," she said. "Let's go around to the back, near the kitchen."

"Good thinking, Kate," Nobby said. "Maybe we'll find another clue." They crept around to the back of the house. The smell was stronger there. It came from an open window. But the window was too high to reach. Nobby found a box and pushed it under the window.

"Let me look first," Kate said. "It's my mystery smell." She climbed up and peeked into the kitchen. "Oh!" Kate said.

"What do you see?" Marsha whispered.

"Let me down!" Kate's eyes were huge. "I saw a ghost!" she told them.

"That's silly," Marsha said. "Let me look." She climbed onto the box.

"What do you see?" Nobby whispered.

Marsha gasped and jumped down. "A wizard!" she said. "Wearing a tall white hat."

"You're both silly," Nobby said. "Let me up there." He took his turn on the box. "Wow!"

"What is it?" Marsha whispered.

"I see the back of a monster. It's pounding something on the kitchen table."

"Shh!" Marsha put a finger to her lips. "Be quiet and listen. It's talking."

A voice was saying, "I'll pound you and thump you hard." There were thumping and bumping sounds. The voice went on. "Now you can rest and get fat, and then into the oven you go." After that it was quiet.

Suddenly, B-A-N-G! The window went down with a slam.

"Run!" Nobby yelled. He raced for the front of the house. Marsha was right behind him.

"Wait for me!" Kate called. They didn't stop running until they were down the street and around the corner.

When they caught their breaths, Marsha said, "Something funny is going on in that house. If we were real detectives, we would go back and find out what it is."

"I guess you're right," Nobby said. He wrote something in the notebook with his pencil.

Then they started back slowly. The haunted house looked even more spooky and empty.

"You can go first this time, Marsha," Kate said.

31

Nobby and Kate followed Marsha onto the porch. She knocked on the door. There was no answer.

"Look," Nobby said. "There's a note pinned to the door."

It said: Please come inside and wait.

"How did it know we were coming?" Nobby said. The hair on the back of his neck began to prickle. Marsha pushed the door, and it squeaked open. The three detectives stood in the middle of a dark room. The mystery smell was very strong. Suddenly they heard a sound.

C-R-E-A-K.

"Who moved?" Marsha whispered.

"I didn't," Nobby said. "Did you, Kate?"

"No," Kate said. "It wasn't me."

All at once they suddenly rushed for the door. Just then someone said loudly, "STOP! DON'T RUN AWAY."

Focus

1. What mystery did Kate bring to Marsha and Nobby?

2. Why didn't Marsha and Nobby believe Kate at first?

3. What made Marsha and Nobby believe there was a mystery later?

4. What do you think the children will do next?

The Mixed-Up Mystery Smell, Part 2

Eleanor Coerr

All of a sudden the lights went on. The detectives looked around. A woman with a rosy face stood near them.

She didn't look

like a wizard or a ghost or a monster. She looked like a chef, with a tall white hat.

"Who are you?" the woman asked.

"We're detectives," Marsha said. "I'm Marsha, and this is Kate. Nobby is our friend."

"I'm Mrs. Birdie," the woman said. "What brings you detectives here?"

"We wanted to find out what makes the mixed-up smell," Marsha told her.

"It's our mystery," Nobby said. "The note on the door said to come in, so here we are."

Mrs. Birdie's face wrinkled into a smile. "That note was for a friend," she said. "But I'm glad you came. I just moved in last week, and I get lonesome. Have you guessed what the smell is?"

"We tried," Nobby answered, "but we didn't have enough clues."

"Then follow me," Mrs. Birdie said. "I'll show you what makes the wonderful smell." She led them down a long dark hall. The warm kitchen was full of the smell. The three detectives stood in the

doorway. They were afraid to look at the table. Then they saw it—the THING on the kitchen table. It didn't look alive. It wasn't even moving. It was a big lump of something brown. Mrs. Birdie pointed to it.

"That's your mystery," she said.

"I know," Marsha cried. "It's bread dough! We read about it at school."

Mrs. Birdie gave each of them some fresh brown bread and butter. It tasted even better than it smelled.

"Then you aren't a wizard," Kate said.

Mrs. Birdie winked. "No, I'm not a wizard, but I do use magic. To bake bread, first you must be happy. If you are grouchy or sad, the bread won't come out right."

"Is that the magic?" Kate asked.

Mrs. Birdie nodded. "That's part of it." Then she showed them how to measure and mix. She showed them how to push and punch and spank the dough. And she told them about
the pinch of

special magic. It was a plant called yeast.

"Yeast makes the dough come alive," she said.

"Then the lump of dough really is alive," Kate said.

"Oh, my, yes," Mrs. Birdie said. "Water and sugar make yeast go sour. This mixture makes gas bubbles in the dough. So the dough grows bigger and bigger." Nobby wrote it all down in his

notebook. Then the detectives went home.

The next morning they met in the clubhouse. The first thing they did was change the sign on the clubhouse door. Now it read: Detectives and bakers at work. Come back later. The second thing they did was make bread. Soon they had a crispy, buttery, mystery smell of their own. It wasn't a mystery any longer!

Focus

1. Who did the wizard turn out to be?
2. What does yeast do to bread dough?
3. To bake bread do you think you would need to know more than this story tells you? Why or why not?

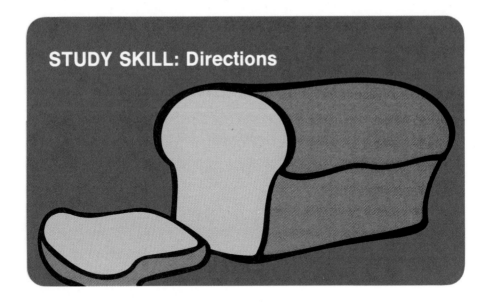

STUDY SKILL: Directions

Kate, Marsha, and Nobby had a good time baking bread with Mrs. Birdie. For the bread to come out right, they had to follow directions. Can you follow directions? Can you give directions for a friend to follow?

Directions often have a title. The title tells you what the directions are about. Sometimes there are pictures to help tell what you should do.

Before you start to follow directions, read all the steps. Make a picture in your mind of what will happen at each step. Think about what you will have when you finish. Make sure you have everything you need.

Sometimes the steps in directions are lettered. Be sure to follow the steps in order. Follow the directions exactly. Even if you skip just one step, something may go wrong.

Look at the directions on the next page. Then answer these questions. Write your answers on a sheet of paper.

1. Why is it important to follow directions step by step?
2. What should you do before you start to follow directions?
3. What do the directions tell you to do first?
4. What would happen if you skipped step B of the directions below?

How to Pour a Glass of Milk

A. Get a carton of milk and put it on the table.
B. Get a glass and put it on the table.
C. Open the carton of milk.
D. Pour the milk into the glass.

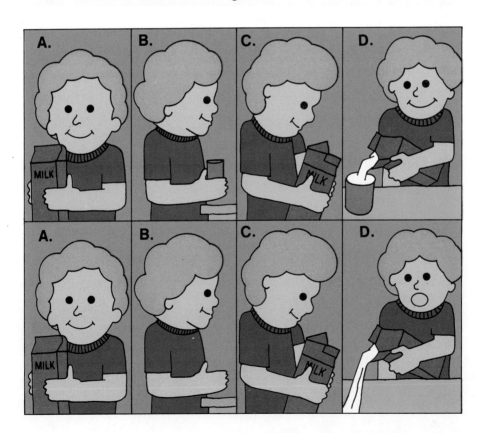

41

Mrs. Birdie taught her new friends how to bake bread. Would you like to try baking some? To make bread rise in the air, read on.

Mrs. Birdie's Bread
Eleanor Coerr

Be happy! If you are sad or grumpy, the bread won't come out right.

First, wash your hands, and put on a big apron.

The first few times you try baking bread, have somebody help you who knows how to bake bread.

You will need: a small saucepan, a big mixing bowl, a small bowl, a measuring cup, a mixing spoon, measuring spoons, a loaf pan, a dish towel, and a baking rack.

Have ready:

dry yeast	wheat germ
brown sugar	cooking oil
milk	whole wheat flour
salt	white flour

1. Put one half cup warm water into small bowl. Slowly sprinkle in 1 package dry yeast and 1 teaspoon brown sugar. Stir gently. Set aside and cover the bowl with a pan or a dish towel.

2. Gently warm one half cup milk in saucepan. Add 2 tablespoons brown sugar and 1 teaspoon salt. Add 3 tablespoons wheat germ, and 2 tablespoons cooking oil. Warm and stir gently until sugar is dissolved. Do not let the milk get hot.

3. Empty saucepan into big bowl. Add one half cup cold water. Add yeast mixture and stir.

4. Stir in 2 cups whole wheat flour. Slowly add 1 cup white flour. Sprinkle flour on your hands. Mix until dough no longer feels sticky. You might have to add about one half cup more flour.

5. Now here comes the fun—kneading. First sprinkle flour on the table and your hands. Kneading means pushing into the dough, then folding it over. Push and fold. Knead the dough for at least 10 minutes—until all the lumps are gone and the dough is smooth.

6. Wash and dry the inside of big bowl. Then rub it with cooking oil. Pat dough into a neat ball

and put it into the bowl. Cover with a dish towel and set aside in a warm place, such as a warm oven that is turned off. Or put it near a warm radiator.

7. Wait for about 1 hour until dough has grown twice as big. Turn it onto the table again. Punch it hard to break all the gas bubbles. Then let dough rest about 5 minutes.

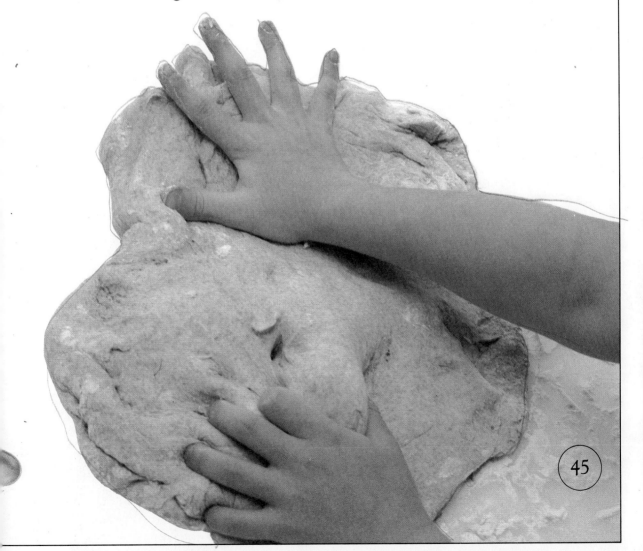

8. Squeeze dough a few times to break any gas bubbles. Pat it into a neat shape to fit into the bread pan. Rub some oil around inside of pan and put dough into it. Cover with dish towel. Set aside in warm place for about one half hour until dough is twice as big.

9. Turn oven to 400 degrees. After 5 minutes put bread into oven. About 30 minutes later, when bread sounds hollow when you tap it, take it out of oven. Run a dull knife between bread and sides of pan. Empty loaf pan onto baking rack to cool.

Now your house has a mystery smell, and you mixed it up yourself, too!

Focus

1. What should you do first when baking bread?
2. Name four things you need to do to make Mrs. Birdie's bread.
3. Name two things that you must do when kneading dough.
4. Think of a new name for "Mrs. Birdie's Bread."

CHECKPOINT

○○○○○

Read these sentences and the words under each. On your paper write each sentence with the word that fits in it.

1. _____ me to the new playing field.

   Follow   Borrow   José

2. Cook the peas in a saucepan for ten _____.

   minutes   magnifying   Marsha

3. _____ the handle came off his cup.

   Charlie   Birdie   Suddenly

4. I'm not sure your dog _____ what to do.

   doughs   understands   kneading

Read the story below. On your paper write the answers to the questions that follow.

The first time I saw the boy he was playing baseball. I wanted to play, too. After the third inning, he came over and asked, "Do you want to take my place?"

"Sure!" I said, and I did pretty well.

After the game was over, the boy cheered. "I'm Sandy," he said. "What's your name?"

"I'm Sandra, but most people call me Sandy." We both laughed. He said, "Welcome to the team."

5. What was the boy doing the first time Sandra saw him?

6. When did Sandra take the boy's place?

7. When did Sandra and Sandy laugh?

Use a word from this list to answer each question below. Write the words on your paper. One word will be left over.

Decoding: Long Words

wisdom   pockets   pointed   singer

8. What is another way of saying *sharp*?

9. What does someone who is wise have?

10. What do most pants have?

Read the directions below. Then, on your paper, answer the questions that follow.

Study Skills: Directions

How to Drink through a Straw

A. Unwrap your straw.

B. Put the straw in your glass.

C. Sip through the straw.

11. What are the directions about?

12. What is the first step?

13. What does the third step tell you?

14. What would happen if you skipped step A?

Do you know the difference between winning and being a winner? Robin knows.

Robin
and the Sled Dog Race
Sara and Fred Machetanz

It was the last three-dog race of the Alaska Snow Fair. Robin Irving went over to her dog Nubby. She rubbed the soft fur behind the dog's ears.

"You're the best leader in the whole world," she told her dog. "We'll make up the time we're behind." Mark Woods's time was two minutes and ten seconds better than Robin's.

51

She looked closely at Nubby's paws to see if they needed care. They were fine. She checked Flip's and Flop's paws. They were fine, too.

As Robin checked her dogs, she thought about the months she had worked to make them a team. She thought back to when they were puppies and

ran beside a team of grown dogs. She remembered the first time they had been put into harness. Nubby had been put beside a leader. That was the way the dogs had learned to go right when she called "gee." They turned left when she called "haw." Robin wanted a well-trained team, so she had worked hard to teach them to follow commands. She had worked them hard with runs to the mailbox miles away every day.

Robin was excited, and the dogs were excited, too. "Whoa, Nubby. Steady, girl, steady." Robin held her dogs. She slipped on the harness. Once in harness, Nubby stood still and held the line straight. Robin harnessed Flip and Flop. Then Robin rode the brake as her father led the dogs to the starting line. They were right behind Mark Woods's team.

Mark's dogs were eager to go, too. Mark and his keeper could barely hold them while the timer counted off the seconds. At the count of "one," Mark's team was off and running.

After a two-minute wait, it would be time for Robin's team to go.

Mr. Irving looked back at Robin. "Just catch up to Mark, and you've made up two minutes. Then you've only ten seconds to go. Good luck!"

The timer began the countdown.

"Five, four, three, two, one!"

"Let's go!" Robin shouted. Nubby and the team sprang forward.

Robin started out running behind the sled. When she was out of breath, she jumped onto the runners. Then she stood on one foot and pushed with the other. As soon as she caught her breath, she jumped off to run again.

Uphill, downhill, and over frozen creeks, Robin ran and drove her team. She came to the evergreen grove, halfway on the three-mile course. Robin could hardly believe it. She didn't feel at all tired.

But Robin began to worry. She was pressing her team more than she ever had. She still had not caught up with Mark.

"Run, Nubby, run, run, run!" she urged. Up the steepest hill Robin pushed until she was panting as hard as the dogs. And then she saw Mark and his team.

Robin could hear the dogs barking and Mark yelling. She saw Mark jump off his sled, turn it over, and run to his leader. Then Robin saw why Mark's dogs had turned off the trail. At the edge of the brush stood a huge moose.

Mark was in a fix. His dogs seemed to be tangled in their harnesses.

"Here's my chance to get ahead," Robin thought. "Let's go, Nubby," she sang out. Then she had another thought. The moose might go after Mark and his dogs. Once Robin thought of that, she knew she had to send help back to Mark. She must, even if it meant she might not win the race.

Across a patch of swamp Robin saw four people.

"Whoa," she called to Nubby and stepped on the brake.

Nubby turned her head. "Why stop?" the dog seemed to ask. "The finish line is just ahead."

"Whoa," Robin repeated. Then she yelled to the people, "Mark Woods's team went after a moose and got tangled up!"

"We'd better go help him," one person said.

"Wait," another shouted. "Here comes Mark now." The people turned to Robin. One yelled, "Get going!"

But Robin was already going. "Run, Nubby, run!" Robin shouted. She jumped off the sled and ran until she could run no longer. She turned for a quick look. Mark was getting closer!

"Faster, Nubby, faster!" Robin cried. She came to the home stretch.

She didn't look back again, but she knew Mark was close. She could hear Mark calling to his team.

Up ahead Robin saw the people watching at the finish line.

They were cheering and yelling and clapping!

Then she heard a voice booming over the loudspeaker. "Here they come now! It's Robin Irving and Mark Woods. The teams are very close. Robin Irving is in the lead. Now Robin is crossing the finish line. This will be a close one. Mark Woods is coming up fast. Mark is over the finish line!"

Robin braked her sled and leaned across the handle. She tried to catch her breath. She had crossed first. But had she made up the time needed to beat Mark and win? The timer didn't say.

Nubby was panting so hard she shook. Robin went to her lead dog and dropped to her knees. She put her arm around Nubby.

"You are the best leader in all the world," she told Nubby. "And you are the best team in the world," she said to Flip and Flop, "even if we don't win."

"Robin!" Robin heard her father's excited voice. "Robin, you won! You won by just two seconds." Mr. Irving hugged Robin. "The best-trained team turned out to be the best team after all, didn't it?"

Robin felt prickly all over. "It really did," she agreed. The best team—that was something she'd believed in and worked for ever since her first "gee" and "haw."

Focus

1. What does this story tell you about? Where does it take place?
2. Tell two things Robin did in training her dogs.
3. What happened to Mark during the race? How did Robin try to help?
4. Was Robin's team really the best trained? Why or why not?

Can you imagine a world without dogs? Dogs, like other animals, make good friends for people. Without them it would be a wagless world. Take a good bark, and read on.

ABOUT DOGS

Margaret Davidson

A long, long time ago, there were no tame dogs. All the animals of the world were wild.

One of those wild animals was the wild dog. Wild dogs roamed through the fields and forests. From these wild dogs have come all the different dogs that are pets today.

How did this happen? It might have begun like this. One day some people were walking in the forest. They found a wild dog that had died. Then they heard a soft mewing sound coming from some thick brush in the forest. Looking around, they saw a wild dog pup curled up in a nest. They picked it up and carried it home.

The pup grew into a full-grown wild dog. The wild dog was now partly tame since it had lived and played with people all its life. Soon people began to raise and train other wild dog pups. Little by little, after many, many years, some of these animals began to look less like wild dogs. These tamer animals were the first pet dogs.

People found that dogs could help them in many ways. Some dogs barked a lot. The loud barking kept robbers and wild animals away. Other dogs could run very fast and help people chase down game. Some dogs helped farmers herd sheep and goats. Dogs helped herd cattle, too. People began to realize that dogs could be useful in different ways. Dogs were also fun to have around.

Since those days, dogs have been trained to do more and more things. Today there are hunting dogs and herding dogs, watch dogs and police dogs. Dogs help to guide the blind. Rescue dogs, sled dogs, and guard dogs help people, too.

Most dogs can't see very well. Anything far away is just a blur to them. But a dog's sense of

hearing is keen. Dogs can hear things that are happening far away. They hear sounds people cannot hear. A dog's best sense is the sense of smell. Some experts say that many dogs can smell many, many times better than people can!

There are many stories of dogs doing brave things. Dogs have helped find lost children. Dogs have saved people from drowning in deep water. They have also saved people trapped in burning buildings.

Dogs will work day and night to please the people they love. Besides good food and water, the only thing a dog needs is a few words of praise or a pat on the head.

Of course, some dogs may be a little too eager to please. One woman trained her dog to go to the street and bring back the newspaper. "Good dog! Good dog!" she said the first time her pet did this alone. Those few words of praise went right to the dog's head. When the woman opened her front door the next morning, she found twenty-three newspapers lying on her porch!

How do dogs do such strange and amazing things? Nobody knows for sure. It is one of the many questions about dogs that people can't answer yet.

But we do know some things about dogs. Dogs seem to be smart and quick. Dogs can be trained to

obey when they are given praise. They dearly love the people they live with, and dogs make wonderful, friendly pets for people who are kind to and care for them.

Focus

1. Where did today's dogs come from? How might they have become tame?
2. Name three ways people of long ago found that dogs could help.
3. Name four kinds of jobs dogs have been trained to do since those days.
4. What is a dog's sharpest sense? How can that sense help people?
5. What is one question about dogs that we can't answer yet?

Flashlight

My flashlight tugs me
through the dark
like a hound
with a yellow eye,

sniffs
at the edges
of steep places,

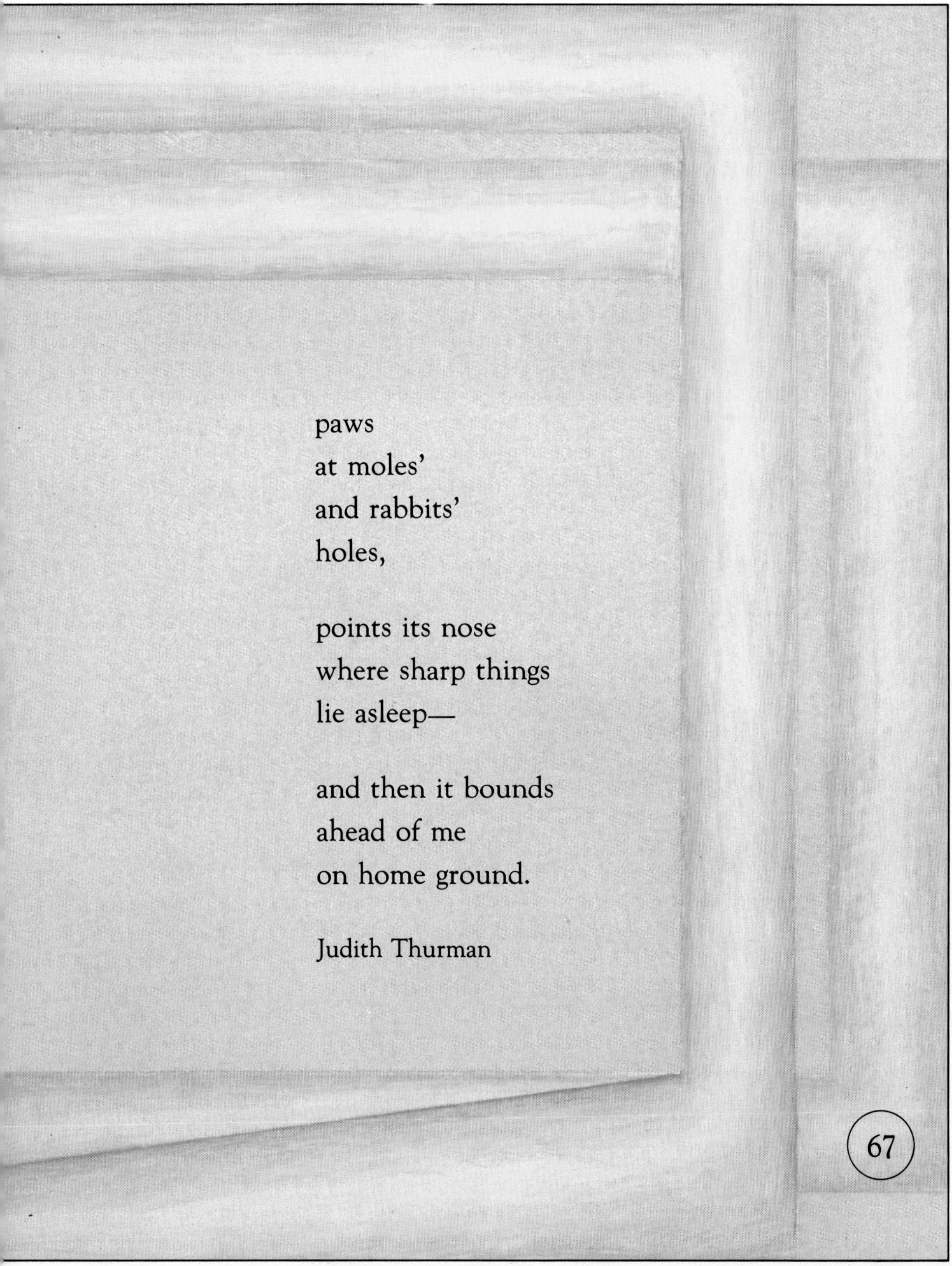

paws
at moles'
and rabbits'
holes,

points its nose
where sharp things
lie asleep—

and then it bounds
ahead of me
on home ground.

Judith Thurman

SCIENCE READING: What's It All About?

It is amazing how much animals can learn from people! We can learn things from animals, too. Science books are filled with facts and ideas about animals. Here are some hints to help you read a science page about animals.

TAKE A FIRST LOOK

Take a first look at the science book page printed here. What different things do you see on this page? What is the title at the top of the page? What will the page be about?

FIND THE KEY IDEAS

Look at the chart on the science page. Make sure you find out what the chart is for. Why, do you think, is one word printed in dark letters? How does this word help you understand the page better?

READ CAREFULLY

Now read the whole page carefully. What is the chart for? You may want to read everything on the page two times. That way you will understand how to use the page. Is the page really about watching animals?

Watching Animals

Watch them at different times of the day. Do they behave in different ways at different times?

   See if you can find out when they are sleepy.

   Find out when they are hungry.

   See what scares them.

   Once you start watching, make some class charts. Make a chart for each animal. The chart may look like this.

KIND OF ANIMAL	
LOCATION	
TIME OF DAY	
BEHAVIOR OF ANIMAL	

   Name the kind of animal.

   Write about where you watched it.

   Write the time of day.

   Write what the animal did.

   If you do something to change the animal's behavior, write what you do. Write how the animal **responds** (ri spond'z).

respond
to react
to
something

69

Did you know that dolphins are part of the whale family? Have you ever seen a dolphin? You may want to see one after you read this "whale of a tale."

ARION

At the edge of the sea, the dolphins waited. They swam back and forth. They dove to the bottom. They broke through the water, chattering to each other.

Arion was the name they spoke. Arion, poet and singer of songs, was the man for whom they waited.

At last they saw him. With his lute under his arm, he hurried to the place where the dolphins swam. He sat upon a stone to tune his lute and plucked each string with his fingers. Then he sang in the full brightness of day. With the sun shining

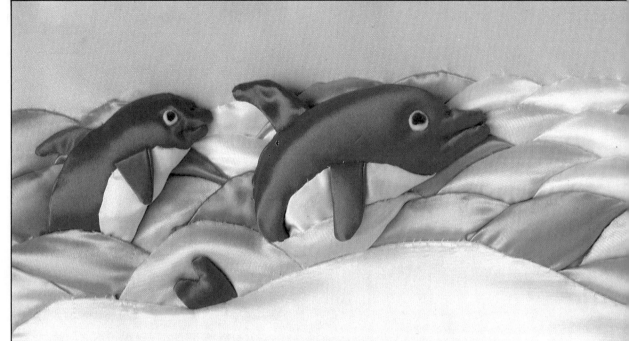

on the sea, he sang. The dolphins leaped from the water. They danced to Arion's music. They dove, and they swam. And Arion made music for them. He was their friend.

Now, Arion was known far and wide as a singer of songs and a fine poet. Everyone knew of him. The children sat at his feet when he sang. It so happened that at this time there was a contest for singers and poets in a far-off land. The people said to Arion that he must go. The queen agreed. No one could sing as sweetly as he. Surely he would win the prize.

So Arion took a ship to the far-off land where the contest was held. Singers and poets from many countries were there. They played their lutes, they

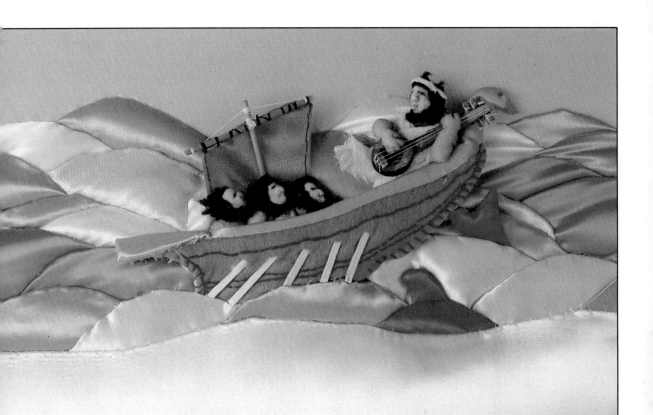

sang of magical places, and each one tried to win the prize. When it came Arion's turn to sing, the people fell silent. Every eye was upon him. Every ear listened.

Arion sang of the sea and the sky. He sang of the dolphins and the sunlight breaking on the waves. When he had finished, the people cheered. Arion had won the contest. He was given the grand prize—a bag of gold.

As soon as he could, Arion took a ship for home. When night fell, he lay down to sleep, his

head resting on the bag of gold. The sea was smooth, and the ship sailed for home. Arion had slept only a short time when he awoke. The sailors were talking softly to each other. From time to time, they looked at Arion to see if he were still asleep. Yet Arion heard what they were saying. In a little while one of them planned to steal Arion's gold! The rest of the sailors would take Arion and throw him into the sea.

When the sailors crept up on Arion, he stood up. "Give us your gold," they cried, "and we will let you have your life." Arion told them that he knew they would throw him into the sea. But he asked one thing of the sailors. "Let me sing one last song," he said. The sailors thought this was fair.

Arion took his lute and looked far out to sea. He lifted his head and sang. Oh, how sweetly he sang! He sang of the sea, and he sang of dolphins. Soon the sea was no longer quiet. Shiny dolphins swam round and round the ship.

At a cry from one of the sailors, Arion was picked up and thrown into the sea. The water and the darkness closed over him. Arion found his dolphin friends and rode off into the night on the back of one of them. By morning he was home in his own land. He hurried to the queen to tell her what had happened. The queen was happy that

Arion had won the prize. But the queen's face grew dark with anger when she learned how Arion lost his gold.

When the sailors' ship came to the land, the queen's guards were waiting. They took the sailors to the queen, who threw them into prison. Arion's prize of gold was given back to him. He thanked the queen, and then he said that he had one more thing to do.

At the edge of the sea, the dolphins waited. They swam back and forth. They broke through the water, chattering to each other. At last Arion came. In the full brightness of day, with the sun shining on the sea, he sang. He sang of his friends the dolphins. He played sweet music on his lute. The dolphins danced for joy.

Focus
1. How did Arion amuse the dolphins?
2. What did Arion do in the far-off land?
3. What did the sailors want more than they wanted Arion's music?
4. Tell how the dolphins helped Arion.
5. Tell what happened to the sailors after they were brought to the queen.

Are dolphins helpful, playful, and friendly only in make-believe stories? Jill Baker wants to tell you that dolphins are wonderful friends in real life, too.

The Friendly Dolphins

Patricia Lauber

The ancient Romans and Greeks knew about dolphins and liked them. Dolphins were pictured on old Roman coins. They were carved in rare gems and painted on walls. There are many tales of dolphins in Greek and Roman poems and stories.

Some of the dolphin tales are made up. They could not have happened. Other tales tell how dolphins played around ships. They helped people who were fishing by driving fish into nets. They saved the lives of swimmers who were drowning. All of these stories may be true. Dolphins do the same things today.

Do dolphins make friends with people? Are the old tales of children and dolphins true? For a long

time it seemed doubtful. Then, in 1955, it did happen. A wild dolphin made friends with a child.

One day a dolphin swam near some boats. People found that the dolphin liked to be scratched gently with an oar. They named her Opo. Opo became even more friendly. She followed the boats! She even began to play with the swimmers.

Opo was willing to play with grown-ups. But she liked children better. She chose to swim among them. Opo made it clear that she wanted to be petted. She picked one child as her special human friend. This was a girl named Jill Baker. If Jill swam

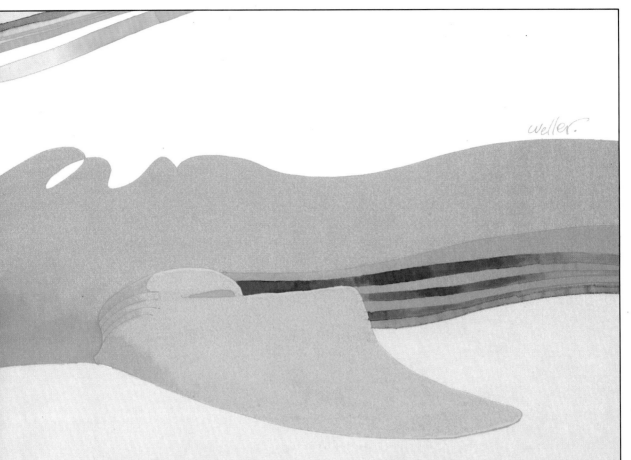

off, Opo followed. Several times the dolphin swam under Jill. Opo picked Jill up and gave her a short ride. Opo would come to Jill for rubbing and petting. She even let Jill put small children on her back.

Opo loved to play. Once someone gave her a beach ball. Opo soon made up a game with it. She tossed it into the air. Then she rushed to the place where it was going to fall. Then she tossed it into the air again! Sometimes she tossed the ball into the air and batted it with her tail.

More and more people came to see Opo. Opo liked it when people laughed or clapped. She would leap out of the water, but not too close to people. Opo was always careful not to harm her human friends. Opo proved that dolphins can be friends with children. This is a rare thing, but it does happen.

Other dolphins have also shown they like people. Free and wild, they have chosen to come near people. They like their human friends. Almost

no other creature of the sea does such a thing. That is one reason many people are interested in dolphins. They seem to like us.

Focus

1. How do we know that early Greeks and Romans knew about and liked dolphins?
2. Why was Opo, the dolphin, rare and special?
3. What is one reason people are interested in dolphins?

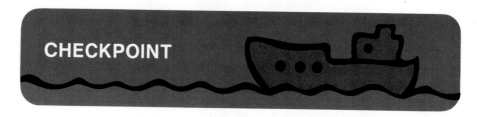

CHECKPOINT

Vocabulary:
Word
Identification

On your paper, write the words from the list below that name things. Then write the words that name people.

Arion   forest   sailors   world
Romans   ship   lute   poet

Vocabulary:
Vocabulary
Development
(homophones)

Complete these sentences using the words below.

nose   heard   hear   see   wood
here   sea   knows   would   herd

1. Can you __see__ the show over everyone's head?
2. Can you __hear__ that bird singing?
3. That clown has a funny-looking _____.
4. I __heard__ a good story the other day.
5. My friend _____ like my telephone number.
6. We use a _____ stove to heat our house.
7. A _____ of cows crossed the road in front of us.
8. I want to stay _____ for a while longer.
9. Dolphins live in the _____.
10. She _____ how to throw a curve ball.

Read the paragraph. Then arrange the sentences below in the right order and write them on your paper.

Tomás got a puppy for his birthday. First he gave his puppy a name. He called it Marcos. Then he taught Marcos to come when called. Next Marcos learned to sit. The next trick Tomás wants to teach Marcos is to stay.

11. a. Marcos learned to sit.

b. Tomás taught Marcos to come.

c. Tomás got a puppy for his birthday.

d. Tomás gave his puppy a name.

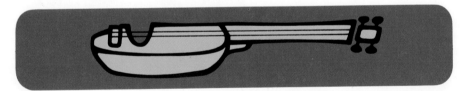

Fill in each blank with a word from the list below. Write each sentence on your paper. One word will be left over.

always   music   borrow   barking   seconds

12. Mark Woods's time was two minutes and ten _____ better than Robin's.

13. Robin could hear the dogs _____.

14. Arion played _____ on his lute.

15. You can _____ tell when someone is your friend.

83

Imagination has wings. With it, people take special trips. They do new things. They make a roller coaster that gives a ride as exciting as any flying machine. They invent things that save lives.

Imagination lets people go back in time. They can watch the first balloon flight in North America. Imagination answers questions. Why is the sky blue? How did the stars come to be? Imagination takes people into the future. Is there life on other planets? How does Earth look to those people?

Using imagination can be pretending. It can be dreaming. But most of all it is wondering. How high *is* the sky?

Welcome to Kansas! It's a hot summer day in the year 1905. Are you dressed to help Amelia? She's making a flying machine, and she needs helpers. But watch out! There's trouble ahead.

Amelia's Flying Machine

Barbara Shook Hazen

Amelia was building a "rolly coaster." Her sister, Murry, and her cousins, Kate and Lucy, were helping. They had been working for many days.

"Back to work," said Amelia.

"Not me," said Kate. "My hand still hurts from yesterday. Besides, I'm sick and tired of doing what you want to do all the time. I quit."

Kate headed toward the house.

"Wait for me," called Lucy. "I'm coming with you."

Murry hung back. "I'll stay," she said. "I'll help."

"Thanks, Murry," said Amelia, giving her sister a hug and a hammer.

Soon they were building again. Amelia and Murry laid a track on the ground. They added more boards until the track was very long. Building the track was hard work. This day seemed even hotter than the day before. Both girls felt wilted and weary.

"Just a little longer," Amelia kept saying. "Just

a few more boards." Amelia and Murry were almost done when cousins Kate and Lucy came back down the path. They were carrying something.

"Lemonade, anyone?" asked Kate. "I'm sorry, Meeley. I didn't mean to get mad. It's just that you're so bossy sometimes."

"I'm sorry, too," said Lucy. "Do you still need help?"

"Just more lemonade," Amelia gulped. "And just in time."

When the lemonade was gone, the girls went back to work. "It looks OK," said Amelia, standing back. "Let's just hope it works."

Kate shook her head. "If Grandma decides to come out here, you're a goner."

"You're right," said Amelia. "And Grandma will tell Father. And he won't take me to the Chicago World's Fair with him. I'll miss my chance to see a real roller coaster."

Murry's eyes grew big. "What are you going to do, Meeley?"

"Hope Jim comes over and hope that Grandma takes that nap," she said, crossing her fingers.

Soon Jim did come over to watch. "I wouldn't miss this for anything," he said with a grin. Amelia made a face at him. Then she turned to her cousins and sister.

Amelia asked, "Shall we draw straws to see who goes first?"

"Not me," said Kate.

"Don't look at me," said Lucy.

Murry shook her head, too. "Not me, Meeley," she said. "But if you go first, I'll keep my fingers crossed."

Amelia carried an apple crate up the ladder to the hayloft and climbed into it. Then she pushed herself partly out of the hayloft window. There she paused and took a deep breath. "It's got to work," she whispered to herself. "It's just got to."

"What are you waiting for?" teased Jim. "Do you want me to try it for you?" Amelia glared at Jim.

"Don't listen to him," yelled Lucy.

"Don't do it," said Kate under her breath. Murry turned her head. She crossed as many fingers as she could. She closed her eyes tight. She didn't want to watch. But she did want to see what was going on. When she opened her eyes to peek, she

91

looked up and screamed, "Stop, Meeley! You can't go!"

The warning came too late. Amelia had just let go. The crate started to roll from the hayloft. As it picked up speed, it went faster and faster down the long track. Amelia felt the speed and the slap of the wind in her face.

"Wow! Look at me," she cried out. "I'm really flying!" The apple crate kept going. It rolled to the end of the track and then onto the ground. Amelia

waved and grinned at Jim as she went by, and he grinned back at her. The crate came to a stop—right by a pair of black-stockinged legs.

"Oh-oh," gulped Amelia, looking up.

Grandmother Otis stared down at Amelia. Her hands were on her hips. Her eyebrows met in a disapproving "V". She spoke in her low we'll-get-to-the-bottom-of-this voice. "Amelia Mary, what are you up to? And what kind of contraption is this?" She tapped her foot. "Amelia Mary, was all this your idea?"

Amelia groaned. Telling the truth meant missing Chicago and the fair and going with her father and everything. "Yes, Gram," she said in a small voice. "It was all my idea." Then she sighed deeply.

"Ma'am," Jim interrupted, "it really wasn't all Amelia's fault. I mean, she made it and rode on it, but I dared her to do it."

Grandmother Otis turned toward Jim. "I might have thought so," she said. "Yes, I might have guessed you were in on this, Jim Watson. Why, I have a mind. . . . "

Amelia bolted to her feet. "But, but Grandma! Jim's not to blame. I'm the one who. . . . "

"I don't want to listen," said Grandma Otis. "Amelia, Murry. Girls. Come with me," she ordered.

"As for you," she stared hard at Jim, "you stay right here and take down this contraption. Right now. Break it up. Every bit of it, mind you." She turned on her heels and headed toward the house.

Amelia hung back. "It isn't fair," she said to Jim. "You're getting the blame. It *was* my idea."

"So what!" Jim shrugged. "You'll get to go to Chicago. She never tells my pa, and she won't tell yours either."

"Know something?" Amelia smiled. "You're really OK."

Jim grinned back. "Just send me a postcard with

something nutty on it like 'Girls can, too!' "

"That's not so nutty," said Amelia. "Someday, Jim Watson, you'll see what a nutty girl can do. Just you wait."

Focus

1. What was Amelia's flying machine? Tell what it was made out of.
2. Why did Amelia agree to be the first to try the machine?
3. How did Jim help Amelia?

95

What a crafty person you are! You always knew it was a good idea to save boxes . . . big, big boxes. Get ready to use your imagination for this project.

Crafty Cardboard Houses

Maurice Pipard

Want a good project for a rainy day? Try starting with a cardboard box and a pair of scissors. Cardboard boxes come in all shapes and sizes. If you are lucky enough, you'll find a clothes washer or freezer box. (You might ask for one at your local department store.)

You will be able to move in right away. Let yourself in by the front door. Use a pair of old scissors. With the scissors cut out a window or two to let in the light. Cut out only three sides of the window. Fold the cardboard back along the fourth side. You can support the hinges and make them stronger with a strip of masking tape. You can try paper and glue, too. Now what kind is your house to be . . . a grocery store, a clubhouse, or a kennel? Let your imagination go wild!

The smaller the cardboard boxes, the more you need. Why not make yourself an igloo? Stack the boxes in layers. Stick them together with tape to keep them from falling down. You can add support to the roof by laying flat wooden slats under the top layer of boxes. Paint the whole thing some color that you really like. Use your imagination. You'll have a wonderful project for rainy days and a warm place in which to dream away a long winter's afternoon.

Focus

1. Where might you find cardboard boxes to use for your house?

2. Name three kinds of houses that can be made with cardboard boxes.

3. Name two things you will need besides boxes for building.

4. Tell how you would use a house made of cardboard boxes.

5. How do you add support to the roof?

LIFE SKILL: White Pages

A cardboard house is fun to make. It can be still more fun to make one with friends. Suppose you want to ask friends to help you. You can call them on the telephone. If you do not know a friend's number, you can find it in the White Pages of the telephone book. You will need to know the name of the adult your friend lives with. The telephone will be listed in this name.

Get the Right Book

There are many telephone books. The numbers for your friend's town may be in a book that has the numbers for people in many towns. Be sure you have the book for the place where your friend lives!

Name, Address, and Number

The White Pages tell you three things about a person:

1. Name
2. Address
3. Telephone number

100

Look at the page from a telephone book printed here. You should notice two things about the names:

1. The names are in alphabetical order.
2. A person's last name comes first.

Look closely at the page. Now see if you can answer these questions. Write your answers on a sheet of paper.

BLOOM—DUVAL

Bloom, Morris 32 Reed St., Beantown 555-4169
Bond, Ann 10 East Fourth St., Willowdale.............555-9127
Brusco, R. F. 30 Bryon St., White Sands 555-0251
Chan, Kee Yip 23 Long Ave., Hollytown................555-3808
Clark, Jane 148 State St., Beantown 555-0230
Costante, Sal 15 Spring St., Peektown..................555-1884
Cox, Diane 413 Ninth Ave., Pleasantville...............555-7725
Diaz, Antonio 969 Broadway, Hollytown................555-6781
Donahue, Sandra 23 Center St., Pinedale.............555-5503
Drew, Peter 49 Tree St., Pinedale 555-6171
Duval, J. D. 6 Glade Ave., Beantown.....................555-5012

1. Name three things that the White Pages tell you about a person.
2. In what order are the names in a telephone book listed?
3. What is Kee Yip Chan's address on the White Page printed here?
4. Which comes first in a telephone book, a person's last name or first name?

I Meant to Do My Work Today

I meant to do my work today—
But a brown bird sang in the apple tree,
And a butterfly flitted across the field,
And all the leaves were calling me.

And the wind went sighing over the land
Tossing the grasses to and fro,
And a rainbow held out its shining hand—
So what could I do but laugh and go?

Richard LeGallienne

103

Do inventors need good imaginations? Think about that as you read about a brave man who turned his imaginings into real-life wonders.

GARRETT MORGAN:
The Wondering Man
John Harmon

At the mouth of the tunnel that day, all was quiet. Workers were deep inside, digging away in the tunnel under the lake. Other workers would arrive soon for the next shift. Suddenly there was a loud explosion! The earth shook. Gases had formed under the lake, and there had been an explosion. Several people ran into the tunnel, but they were driven back. No one could breathe. In 1916 there were no gas masks.

"Get Garrett Morgan!" someone cried. In all of Cleveland, he was the one man who might help. Garrett had invented something called a Safety Hood. Someone went after him. Soon Garrett and his brother Frank were at the tunnel. They put on their Safety Hoods and bravely walked right into the tunnel.

Soon they both came out, each carrying one of the trapped workers. The waiting crowd cheered. Many people wept. Again and again, Garrett and Frank went back into the tunnel. They saved thirty-two people.

For being so brave, Garrett Morgan was given a gold medal. The explosion at the tunnel had proved one thing: a Safety Hood was a good idea! It saved many lives.

How did Morgan get the idea for the Safety Hood? A story in a newspaper may have started the idea. Morgan was reading about three fire fighters who had died in a bad fire. They had been breathing smoke.

"I wonder if they could have been saved?" Garrett wondered. But Garrett did more than wonder. He searched for an answer. Perhaps something could stop the smoke or gas and still let a person breathe. Garrett tried a number of ideas. He searched until he came up with an answer. His answer to saving the fire fighters was the Safety Hood. Today we would call it a gas mask. Garrett Morgan made the first successful one in our country.

Do you ever wonder how someone gets to be an inventor? How did Garrett Morgan become an inventor? Perhaps it was because he never stopped wondering.

When Garrett was a boy, he liked school. He liked learning, and he liked to think. He was curious about everything—how it worked, how it might work better. But Garrett had to leave school after the sixth grade to go to work. Many young children had to work in those years. Their families

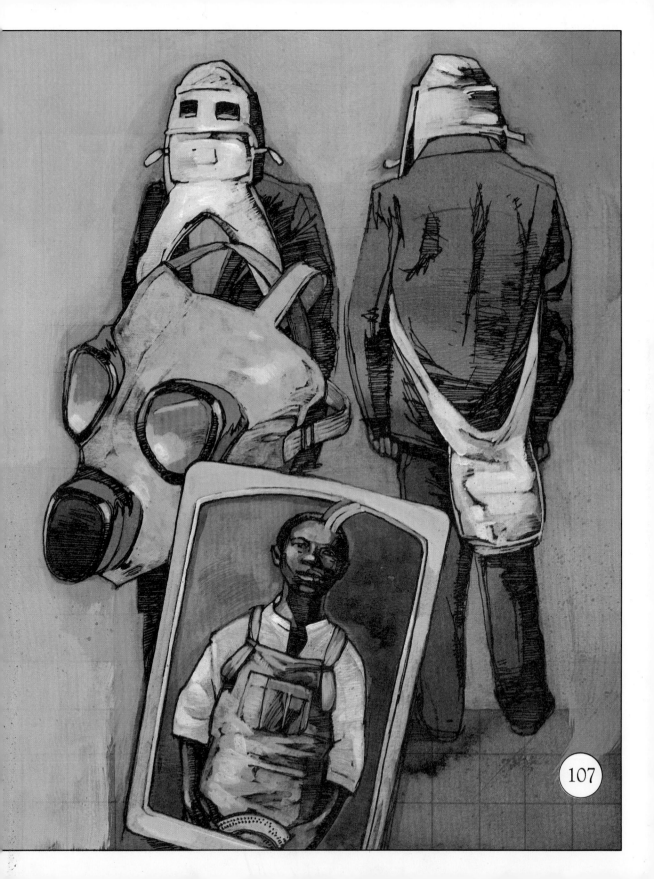

needed the money.

When Garrett was fourteen years old, he left home. He wanted to live and work in the city. "The city is where things happen," he told his parents.

When he got to Cleveland, Garrett had only ten cents in his pocket. He wasn't worried, though. He was a hard worker, and he knew he would find a job. One day Garrett met a man who owned a company that made sewing machines.

"I've pulled machines apart," Garrett told the owner. "I've put them back together, too." Garrett got a job with the sewing machine company. He worked hard and learned all he could.

In four years, Garrett was able to start his own repair shop for sewing machines. During all these years, Garrett Morgan never stopped wondering.

In a few years, Garrett's shop had done so well that he bought a house. Soon after that, he married Mary Anne Hassek. They were very happy. Garrett kept on working in his repair shop. He also kept on wondering. One day, Garrett went for a drive. He came to a crossroad just in time to see an accident. A car and a horse-drawn wagon had crashed into each other.

Garrett wondered why one of the drivers hadn't stopped. He also knew that soon there would be many more cars on the road. There had to be some way to tell drivers when to stop and when to go. Garrett wondered.

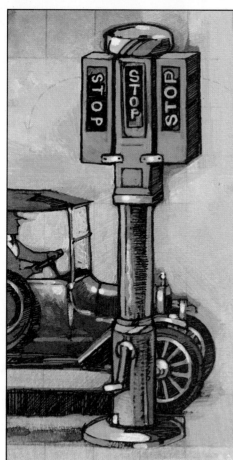

That night Garrett made some drawings. They were of a traffic signal. When the stop signal showed on one side, it told drivers who saw it to stop. When it showed on the other side, the drivers could go.

Garrett sold his invention, and it became our first traffic signal. Today we could not get along without traffic signals. The next time you see a traffic signal, think of Garrett Morgan.

Garrett Morgan lived a long and happy life. He invented many things that people needed. He did this because he wondered. Garrett Morgan wondered about things all his life.

Focus

1. Why did people begin to use Garrett's masks?
2. What was Garrett Morgan's first job?
3. What gave Garrett the idea for traffic lights?
4. What did Garrett do that helped him invent new things?

Have you ever left your homework at home? Well, Stuey brought his to school, but he still didn't have it. Find out why.

The Case of the MISSING HOMEWORK

Lilian Moore

Stuey filled his fountain pen. He took a clean white sheet of paper and wrote carefully. Nothing but faint pink lines appeared on the paper. Then he held the paper close to the big light bulb of his desk lamp.

As if by magic, clear blue words began to show. In a little while there was the urgent message: Report at once to Agent X. The password is Abracadabra.

Stuey moved the paper away from the heat of the bulb. Slowly the words began to disappear.

"This is super!" he cried. "Just what I want!" Stuey's plan was simple. He was going to sell invisible ink.

"I'll make enough of this ink to fill all my ink bottles," he said to himself. "I'll bet lots of my friends will want some. Then we can send each other secret messages!"

But Stuey did not have a chance to talk about his ink in school the next day. Ms. Taylor called him to her desk. There lay the last two pages of homework Stuey had done. The papers were full of

red lines and circles.

Ms. Taylor had *not* been able to read what Stuey had written. What was more, she didn't think anybody could. She made it clear that Stuey would have to do his homework more carefully, or do it over. "Every time!" said Ms. Taylor.

It was a cold and windy day. By the time school was over and Stuey got home, it was much too cold to work in his lab out in the back shed.

Stuey sighed. He'd have to make his ink tomorrow. Meanwhile, he had better get to his homework and get it over with.

The radiator in his room made a nice cozy sound. It was like the purr of a happy cat. Stuey

pulled his chair over and warmed his cold feet.

"Say, this feels good," he told himself.

He reached for his books and paper and fountain pen. He leaned on the warm radiator. He then began his work very carefully.

When he finished he looked at his paper proudly. He had even made his g's and his y's with fancy-looking twists. "Ms. Taylor should be able to read this!" he thought.

Stuey gathered up his books. He packed his sneakers for gym the next day. He was all ready to put his homework into his loose-leaf notebook. He looked around, puzzled. He had put his homework on the desk with his books and the pack of loose-

leaf paper. He knew he had. But he did not see the homework!

Stuey looked under the desk. It was not there either. Maybe it was mixed up with all the things on his desk. He moved all the papers and books from his desk to his table. The homework was not on his desk. He moved everything from his table to the bed. It was not on the table. He moved everything from the bed to the floor. Frantically he looked under the bed. Where could his homework *be*? Then he moved the books and papers off the floor. With a cry of relief, he saw his homework!

"Whew!" he said, talking to the paper in his hand. "You had me worried!" This time he put the

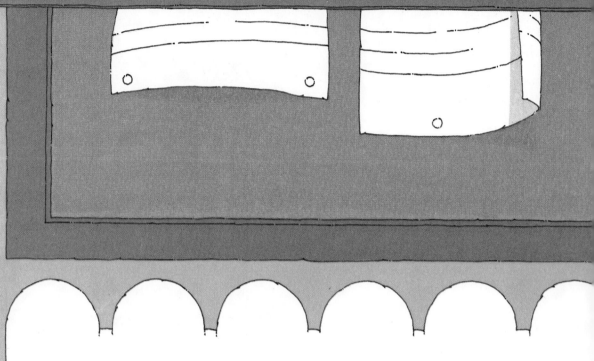

homework carefully into his notebook. Just to make sure he would find it quickly the next day, he put a clip on top of the page.

Ms. Taylor usually had the class hand in homework at the beginning of the day. It was passed to the first person in each row. Then it was all collected.

That morning, Ms. Taylor said, "Stuey, please let me see your work before it is collected."

Stuey puffed out his chest just a little. He thought of the surprise he had for Ms. Taylor. He flipped open his notebook. The clip was there, all right. But where was his homework? Stuey leaned forward and took a good look at the paper. To his

horror, he saw faint pink lines.

"Stuey," said Ms. Taylor, "I'm waiting."

Stuey stood up. He looked from his notebook to his teacher. "Ms. Taylor," he began, swallowing hard, "I made an awful mistake. . . ."

"Do you have your homework today, Stuey?" Ms. Taylor asked. Stuey walked up to the front of the room. He laid the paper on Ms. Taylor's desk.

"I did do my homework, Ms. Taylor," he said quickly. "I really did! But I guess I used the wrong pen. I . . . I did it in invisible ink!"

The whole class was suddenly quiet.

"Stuey," said Ms. Taylor, "is this your idea of a joke?"

At that moment, Stuey heard the soft purring of the radiator beside Ms. Taylor's desk. "Look, Ms. Taylor!" he said. He picked up the paper and laid it on the radiator. Silently he spoke to his homework. "Please come back . . . just once more!" Slowly the words began to appear.

Ms. Taylor looked at the paper. "This is very careful work, Stuey," she said. "It's too bad you didn't do last week's homework in disappearing ink!"

"Mom!" cried Stuey the next afternoon. "Guess what!"

"I give up," said his mother.

"I made seventy-five cents! I sold all the invisible ink I could make . . . seven bottles for a dime each and half a bottle for a nickel. Everybody wanted some ink after seeing my homework!"

Focus

1. What did Stuey invent? What was he going to do with it?
2. Stuey's ink nearly got him into trouble with Ms. Taylor. Tell how.
3. How did Stuey show Ms. Taylor that he had done his homework?
4. Why do you think people bought Stuey's invisible ink?

CHECKPOINT

On your paper write the complete sentences below. Choose the best word from the list for each blank.

1. I like _____ better than grape drink.

   ordered   invisible   lemonade   radiator

2. Cutting paper with _____ is not always easy.

   signal   scissors   searched   support

3. Amelia wanted to go to the _____ World's Fair.

   Stuey   Garrett   Chicago   Otis

4. They lived in a _____ made of brick.

   sewing   building   hinges   answer

Read the paragraph below. Then choose the sentence that tells the main idea. Write the sentence on your paper.

Toby had no money, but he wanted to give his mother a present. "What could I do for her?" he wondered. He knew she hated to sew. So all week he mended clothes. He sewed patches over holes. He replaced buttons. Then he laid the clothes in a box and tied a ribbon around it. Toby's mother said it was the best present she had ever gotten.

5. What is the main idea of the paragraph?

   a. Toby needed a present for his mother.

   b. Mother hated to sew.

   c. Toby liked to sew.

   d. The clothes needed to be mended.

Fill in each blank with a word from the list at the right. Write the sentences on your paper.

Decoding: Vowels with *r* (*er, ir, or, ur*)

6. Juana did not know what the ring was _____.   fur

7. My parents are _____ if I break the rules.   worth

8. Cats have soft _____.   stern

Use the sample telephone book page below to answer the questions that follow. Write your answers on your paper.

Life Skills: Resources (telephone directory)

> **Jannita, Jane** 104 Maple Dr., Teatown 555-6084
> **Johnson, G.** 16 Sumac Pl., Carrotville...................555-6201
> **Julla, Jack** 11 Sea Ave., Potatotown.....................555-2382

9. How is a person's name listed in the telephone book?

10. What does the telephone book tell you besides a person's telephone number?

Can a dog fly like a bird? Well, it's Philadelphia in 1793. Our young country is full of imaginative happenings . . . and people . . . and one dog named Toby.

THE FIRST BALLOON FLIGHT IN NORTH AMERICA

Edmund Lindop

Boom! A cannon thundered in the cold morning air.

Boom! A second cannon blast shook the bed on which Roger Wallace and his dog, Toby, were sleeping.

Roger awoke and his heart pounded with excitement. This was the day when a man would climb into a balloon and try to fly!

Other people had tried balloon flights in our country. They had all failed. Today, another person would try to soar high above the trees. His name was Jean Pierre Blanchard, and he had come all the way from France.

Tickets were sold for seats in the courtyard where Mr. Blanchard would begin his flight. The tickets cost five dollars each . . . a lot of money. But Roger just had to see Mr. Blanchard take off in his balloon! So Roger had spent long hours working for his friend, Mr. Bowen. By the day of the flight he had saved enough money.

Now, as he ran down the cobbled street, Roger thought of flying. What a thrill to go soaring up, up, up!

Roger soon saw Mr. Bowen in the crowd and waved to him. "Good morning, sir," he called. "Is Mr. Blanchard ready?"

"He should be," Mr. Bowen answered. "I'm sure my friend came very early to get ready."

Roger's eyes were filled with excitement. "I wish I could go up with him."

The man thought for a while. He knew the boy wanted to fly. He smiled. "Mr. Blanchard's balloon can take only one person in the air, but what would you think if he took your dog?"

"Take Toby!"

"Yes," Mr. Bowen replied. "To tell you a secret, I think Mr. Blanchard would like some company."

Mr. Bowen patted Toby's small head. "How do you feel about it?" he asked. "Do you want to be the first dog in Philadelphia to fly?"

Toby barked. He seemed to know that Mr. Bowen's words were important.

Carrying Toby in his arms, Mr. Bowen pushed through the crowd with Roger at his side. They walked over to the balloonist, and Roger shook hands with Mr. Blanchard. The boy's heart beat fast.

Mr. Bowen talked with the balloonist for a few minutes. Roger could not understand what they said because they spoke in French. But when his friend handed Toby over, Roger knew his little dog was going to have a great adventure.

All of a sudden the band stopped playing. The cannons roared again. This time it was a fifteen-gun salute. That could mean only one thing. President George Washington was coming! People cheered. The President stepped into the courtyard. He shook hands with Mr. Blanchard, the French balloonist, and handed him a paper. It was an official letter. Mr. Blanchard did not speak English. The letter would help him tell people what he was doing.

All was ready. Mr. Blanchard climbed in with Toby under his arm. He ordered the ropes to be freed. Soon the balloon rose and was caught in a strong breeze. Never had anyone gone so fast!

Through the clouds and out of sight sailed the balloon. Mr. Blanchard was happy. He gave Toby a

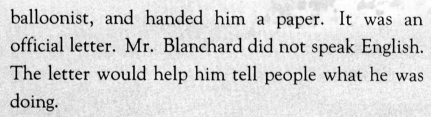

127

friendly pat. They had climbed high into the sky, and all was going well! Blanchard took a short rest. He looked at the view.

All of a sudden danger struck! From the south a thick fog was coming. This could mean real trouble. Blanchard would not be able to see in the fog, and the balloon might drift out to sea. The balloonist knew that he must act quickly. He had to land the balloon before the fog blinded him.

128

He opened a valve. The big yellow ball began floating down. The fog swirled around the balloon, and Mr. Blanchard couldn't see the land below. But between the waves of fog, he caught a glimpse of a small clearing. Holding his breath, his heart pounding, he clung on. Finally the balloon came skidding to rest in a meadow.

Mr. Blanchard and Toby were completely lost. But then two men and two women came by on horseback. They read the President's letter and were eager to help Blanchard. Soon they all started back to Philadelphia.

Finally they arrived! Roger raced to Toby.

"How does it feel to fly like a bird?" he asked, holding the dog in his arms. "The next time you go flying, I'm going, too!"

Focus

1. What was one thing Roger wanted to do?
2. Why was Roger not allowed to fly in the balloon?
3. Who finally got to fly with Mr. Blanchard?
4. What danger did Mr. Blanchard and his friend face in the flight?
5. What was special about this balloon flight?

STUDY SKILL: Maps

Imagine looking down from Mr. Blanchard's balloon. The picture and map on the next page show what you might see. They both show the same scene, even though they look different.

Maps Use Symbols

In the picture, you can see trees and a railroad. The map uses symbols to show the same things. This map has a chart called a key. The key tells you what the symbols mean.

Find the key on the map on the next page. What symbol stands for a railroad? Find this symbol on the map. Then look at both the map and the picture. Is the map symbol for railroad in the same place as the real railroad in the picture?

Maps Show Direction

Another symbol on the map shows directions. This symbol is called a direction finder. North is at the top of the map. West is at the left. Where are south and east?

Look at the map on the next page. Answer these questions on a sheet of paper.

1. Where would you look to find the map symbol for a forest? Draw it.

2. What symbol on the map helps you find north?

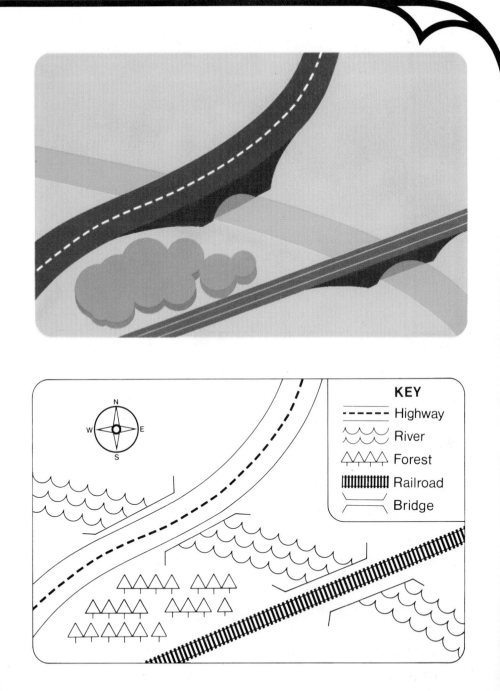

Can you imagine what makes the sky blue? A scientist and a poet each tell why.

IS THE SKY REALLY BLUE?

Susan Hadfield

Is the sky blue? Take a look right now. Is it really blue? If it were a cloudy day, the sky would

not be blue. It would be dark and gray. If it were late in the afternoon, the sky might not be blue. It might be red, pink, orange, even purple. If it were a bright, bright day, the sky might not be blue. It might be almost white. But it is blue sometimes, maybe most of the time. Why?

The answer comes from the sky and the sun. (But don't look at the sun! It would hurt your eyes.) Light comes from the sun, of course. But this

133

light is white when it starts its journey from the sun to the earth. The white light of the sun is made of every color . . . orange, red, yellow, green, blue, and violet. When the light reaches earth, it hits the layer of air that surrounds all of us. The light has to pass by all the things that are in the air, such as the clouds, bits of dust, and pollution. The white light gets scattered.

When the sun is high in the sky in the middle of the day, only the blue light gets through all the things in the air. But as the sun starts to go down, different colors are able to get through the air. That is why at sunset we can sometimes see beautiful reds, oranges, yellows, and purples in the sky.

But why is the sky blue and not yellow or green instead? See if *you* can come up with a good answer.

135

Why the Sky is Blue

I don't suppose you happen to know
Why the sky is blue? It's because the snow
Takes out the white. That leaves it clean
For the trees and grass to take out the green.
Then pears and bananas start to mellow,
And bit by bit they take out the yellow.
The sunsets, of course, take out the red
And pour it into the ocean bed
Or behind the mountains in the west.
You take all that out and the rest
Couldn't be anything else but blue.

—Look for yourself. You can see it's true.

John Ciardi

Focus

1. Name two colors other than blue that the scientist says the sky might be.

2. According to the scientist, what color is light when it comes to earth from the sun?

3. What colors did the poet say were taken out of the sky? What one color was not taken out?

What do you think stars are made of? Does "twinkle, twinkle little diamond" sound right to you? Read this tale for a make-believe answer.

The Sack of Diamonds

Helen Olson

Many years ago the sky had no stars, as it does now. One day a woman who lived alone, except for her dog, had her one hundredth birthday.

The townspeople rejoiced with her in the town square. There was much feasting and dancing in the streets. Then, to the surprise of everyone, the king himself appeared. The king gave the woman a sack of diamonds for her birthday.

"Oh, me! Oh, my!" said the woman. "What a rare gift, a sack of diamonds! They are very pretty."

"Yes, indeed," cried the people. "What a rare and valuable gift!"

Then the sun began to set, and the woman bid the others good-by. The woman hurried home with her sack of diamonds and her dog. She did not want to be out too late. Unless the moon was out, the

starless nights were very dark indeed.

The next morning the woman sat in her little chair in her little house. The woman thought about what to do with the sack of diamonds.

"It is a rare gift, indeed," she said to her dog. "But I already have everything I need. I have my little house, my garden, and my warm cloak, which will last for many a year."

Suddenly she jumped up from her chair. "Here I am sitting," she said, "when I should be up and about. I must hide this pretty treasure so it will be safe from robbers."

No sooner had she said this than she dug a hole in her garden and covered over the sack of diamonds. But the dog immediately dug them up and brought them back to the woman.

"Oh, me! Oh, my!" said the woman. "This will never do."

Next she hid them in the well. But when she took a drink of water, it tasted sour because of the sack.

"Oh, me! Oh, my!" said the woman. "The chimney . . . I will hide the sack of diamonds in the chimney!"

However, when she started a fire all the smoke came into the house. The diamonds had stopped up the chimney.

"I cannot stand this," said the woman. "I will have to think of something else." She strapped the sack on her back. But her back ached so much from the weight that she soon had to take the sack off.

"Oh, me! Oh, my!" she said. "What to do? What to do?" And she sat down on the sack of diamonds, but it was so uncomfortable that she soon had to get up.

"I wish I were rid of these diamonds," she said

141

to her dog. "They have caused me nothing but trouble."

The first thing next morning the woman loaded the sack into her wheelbarrow. She pushed the wheelbarrow to the town square. There she left her burdensome treasure. Then she returned home with the empty wheelbarrow.

"Oh, me! Oh, my!" she told the dog. "How glad I am to be rid of those diamonds!"

Just then there was a knock on the door. Some townspeople were standing on the doorstep. They set down the sack of diamonds.

"We have found the sack of diamonds the king gave you," they said. "It was in the town square."

"Imagine that!" said the woman.

After the townspeople had left, the woman shook her head.

"Oh, me! Oh, my!" she said. Then she opened the sack and looked at the diamonds. They sparkled and sparkled.

"The diamonds are pretty," she said to the dog, "but they are of no use to me."

Then she sat down in her chair, put her chin in her hand, and thought and thought.

Suddenly she jumped up. "Oh, me! Oh, my!" she said. "Now I know what else I can try. Why didn't I think of it sooner?"

She set to work immediately. Soon she had finished making a fine, strong slingshot. It was pitch dark outside, as it was most nights. Then with

her slingshot, the woman shot one diamond after another into the dark sky. There the diamonds stayed, making the night sky bright.

By the time she had gotten rid of the whole sack of diamonds, the sky was filled with twinkling lights. The diamonds still twinkle away to this very day. The woman was well pleased with herself.

"Now the diamonds are of use to everyone," she said to her dog. "Now I can have joy in my life without that sack of diamonds cluttering up my house!"

Focus

1. Why did the king give the woman a sack of diamonds?

2. The woman was not happy with the diamonds. Why?

3. List four ways the woman tried to get rid of the diamonds.

4. What did the woman finally do with the diamonds? Was she happy then? Why or why not?

Imagine you're on a spaceship. Where would you go in outer space? Who—or what—might meet you when you land? (You had better travel with a friend.)

Our World Is Earth

Sylvia Engdahl

I like to pretend I'm in a spaceship, don't you?

Suppose we were traveling in a spaceship far, far out in space—almost as far as the moon. Suppose we met a ship full of space people. And suppose they asked us where our home is.

"Our world is planet Earth," we'd say.

But suppose the space people hadn't traveled to Earth? What would we say then?

"Earth is a world with blue skies and yellow sunlight," we'd say. "The sun is fiery bright, too bright to look at, but you can see its light touch everything.

"It often shines on us. We feel its warmth when

we're outdoors, with warm air all around us. The sun feels good on our skin.

"There are days when we don't see sunlight. Clouds stretch across the sky . . . white billowing clouds, gray mottled ones, or dark clouds that hold rain. Sometimes rain mists down slowly. Sometimes it falls in sheets, splashing on highways and turning dirt roads to mud. Rain soaks into the ground. It fills rivers and lakes and oceans. Earth is a world of water as well as sunlight.

"When the wind blows the clouds away, the sun appears again. It has been shining all the time above the clouds."

That's what we'd say to the space people. I wish we could meet them, don't you? I like Earth's sunlight. I like Earth's fresh, cool rain. I like to look up into blue skies or cloudy ones. But I like the night sky, too! At night I look up at glimmering points that dot the darkness. I think about other worlds.

We look up at the stars and know they are suns. There are suns that give yellowish light, as ours does, or bluish light, or reddish light . . . beautiful suns of many kinds. I wonder if their light shines on worlds. Do other suns have worlds like Earth? Nobody knows. I mean nobody on planet Earth yet

knows. Maybe, if there are worlds near those suns, there are people on them who know.

Maybe, near faraway suns, there are some worlds with people. When we pretend we're talking to space people, we have to guess how they look. Perhaps people of far-off suns' worlds aren't like people of our world. They may not be the same size. They may not even be the same shape!

We can't imagine what they look like. Most likely they can't imagine what we look like, either. I wonder if their planets have rivers and forests and fields like Earth's, or if everything there is different.

I wonder if they have great cities. I wonder if we'll ever know.

Focus

1. What does the author of this story like to pretend?

2. Suppose you were a space traveler and had never seen Earth. Would this story help you know what Earth was like? Why or why not?

3. Why does the author like Earth's daylight? Why does she like Earth's night?

4. When the author looks at stars, what does she wonder?

CHECKPOINT

Vocabulary:
Word
Identification
Answer each question by using one of the words from the list below it. Write the word on your paper.

1. Which word means "to make a picture in your mind"?

imagine   planet   twinkle   pretty

2. Which word names a rare gem?

cannons   wheelbarrow   diamond   heart

3. Which word names our planet?

Earth   Orange   Suppose   Blanchard

Vocabulary:
Vocabulary
Development
(context clues)
Read the sentences below. Choose the correct word to fill in each blank. Write the completed sentences on your paper.

4. The people were _____ because their team had won.

gray   juicy   rhinoceros   cheerful

5. He read the problem many times, but he was still _____ by it.

loved   saved   supposed   puzzled

Read the story. Then write two sentences from the list that tell about the underlined main idea.

Comprehension: Supporting Details

Clouds pile up in the sky over the land. <u>They are made from water in the air</u>. The water comes from oceans, lakes, and rivers. The warm sun shines on the water. The heat from the sun changes some of the water into mist. Then these tiny bits of mist float into the sky and join to make clouds.

6. a. Clouds pile up in the sky over land.

b. Clouds get water from oceans.

c. Clouds are often big and dark.

d. Warm sunshine changes water into mist.

Fill in each blank with a word from the list. On your paper write each sentence.

Decoding: Vowels with *r* (*er, ir, or, ur*)

person   swirled   worth   termed

7. That _____ is ten years old.

8. The leaves _____ directly at him.

9. How much is the old coin _____?

153

Story

Storytellers

Everyone is a storyteller. We tell stories all the time! "Remember the time when . . . ?" Have you told a story that starts that way?

Some stories are true. Some are made up. The stories on the next pages are all old favorites. The story that tells how the rhinoceros kept its skin is made up. The story about Winnie-the-Pooh is, too. One story tells about the way some animals really act. Is it fact or fiction? Another tells about the life of a famous writer.

Remember, everyone is a storyteller. Have *you* told a good story lately?

tellers

Every day people give, and they receive. But do they always get what they deserve?

WHAT · HE DESERVES

ACT 1 Helen L. Howard

Characters:

NARRATOR

QUEEN AND KING, the rulers of the land

PAGE, a child who serves the Queen and King

FARMER, a poor woman

RICH BROTHER

TWO GUARDS, who guard the castle

NARRATOR: A Queen and King much loved by their people are seated in the throne room. There is a guard at each side of the throne. The Queen and King are talking.

KING: How good it is to be at peace again! Our country is rich, and our people seem happy.

QUEEN: Our people are thankful to us for our leadership. The presents they give us prove this.

KING: I am grateful to our people for their gifts. (*A page enters.*) Page, you seem to be in a hurry. Do you have a message? Does someone need us?

PAGE: No, Your Majesty. A farmer comes. She has a gift for you.

QUEEN: Even the farmers bring gifts!

KING: Let her come in so that we may thank her in person. My Queen, another gift. How pleasing to have the farmers so generous!

PAGE: Here is the giver, Your Majesties.

KING: My page tells me that you have brought us a gift. We are very pleased that you thought of us.

FARMER: Your Majesty, I am only a poor farmer, but when I harvested my turnips, I found one so large that it would hardly go into my cart. I said to my husband, "Why, this is a turnip fit for the Queen and King!" So, Your Majesties, I have brought it to you.

KING: A turnip larger than a cart! Where is this wonderful vegetable?

FARMER: It is in the courtyard, Your Majesty. It would hardly go through the gate.

QUEEN: Let us see this remarkable turnip!

FARMER: If you will look through the window, you can see it in the courtyard.

KING: Look! I have never seen such a sight before! It is indeed larger than a cart.

QUEEN: The cart is bending under its weight. It is a heavy load for two strong horses.

FARMER: Yes, Your Majesty. My one horse could not pull

KING: it, so I borrowed one of my neighbor's horses.

KING: Such a gift deserves a reward. What shall we give her?

QUEEN: A bag of gold and jewels would help her most, no doubt.

KING: Page, bring me a bag of gold and jewels. We have decided to reward you, my honest friend. Here is a bag of gold and jewels in return for your gift.

FARMER: Oh, thank you, Your Majesties! I can hardly believe my good fortune. Why, there is enough here to buy food and clothing for my good husband and me for the rest of our lives. You are most generous! I must be off to tell my husband.

QUEEN: Guard, follow that farmer, but do not let her see you.

NARRATOR: It is now a few minutes later. The guard is hiding by a clump of bushes watching the farmer.

GUARD: Here comes the farmer now. I'll just hide here and wait until she passes; then I can follow her.

FARMER: A whole bag of gold and jewels! After I pay my neighbor for his horse, I will still have more gold and jewels than I ever dreamed of.

NARRATOR: As the farmer is looking at her riches, her rich brother approaches. He is walking with his nose in the air. The rich brother bumps into the farmer, and drops his cane and his high hat.

RICH BROTHER: (*Angrily*) Here, you farmer! Why don't you look where you are going? Must we always be annoyed by you farmers walking along the same road with us?

FARMER: Oh, sir, I'm sorry!

RICH BROTHER: Well, if it isn't my poor sister! Where have you been in your ragged coat?

FARMER: I've been to the palace.

RICH BROTHER: To the PALACE! What have you been to the palace for? I suppose the Queen and King sent you a special invitation!

FARMER: I took the Queen and King a present. Just see what they gave me in return.

RICH BROTHER: A bag of gold and jewels! What in the world did you give them that they gave you such a present?

FARMER: I gave them a turnip.

RICH BROTHER: A turnip! You gave the Queen and King a turnip, and they made you rich!

FARMER: Yes. I must hurry home and tell my husband and neighbors of our good fortune. (*The farmer rushes off.*)

RICH BROTHER: Hah! The Queen and King are, without doubt, too generous! . . . I have an idea. If the Queen

161

and King give a bag of gold and jewels for a mere turnip, what would they give for a truly fine present! Now let me see . . . what do the Queen and King like best of all? I have it . . . horses! The Queen and King love their horses and spend a lot of time at the royal stables. I'll use my whole fortune to buy the Queen and King some fine horses. Then we shall see who is the best-rewarded giver in the kingdom! No doubt the Queen and King will make me a noble . . . indeed, the wealthiest noble in the land!

NARRATOR: The guard, you remember, has been listening.

GUARD: This is information for the Queen. I'll return to the palace and tell her.

Focus

1. What made the farmer think her turnip was a good present for the Queen and King?
2. What was the farmer's reward?
3. Why did the farmer receive the reward?
4. What is the rich brother planning to do now? Why?
5. In a play, who tells you what happens between the scenes?

WHAT · HE DESERVES

ACT 2

Helen L. Howard

NARRATOR: And now a few hours later, back in the throne room of the palace, the guard is talking with the Queen. The King is looking out of the window. He sees something unusual in the courtyard. Listen.

KING: What a sight! Just coming into the courtyard are a dozen of the finest horses I have ever seen. Can it be that someone is making us another gift?

GUARD: Your Majesties, it is he, the rich man.

QUEEN: How quickly he has sold his land and bought the horses! He is as eager as he is generous!

KING: Such a generous gift must be well rewarded. My Queen, you must think of an unusual and special gift for this worthy man.

QUEEN: Yes, indeed! He shall receive the gift he deserves!

PAGE: A fine gentleman desires to see you, Your Majesties. He has brought you a gift.

KING: Let him enter at once. Have you thought of a reward for him, my dear?

QUEEN: Yes, he shall receive what he deserves!

RICH BROTHER: Your Majesties, I have brought you a gift.

KING: Can it be all of those splendid horses I saw coming into the courtyard just now?

RICH BROTHER: Yes, Your Majesty. I wanted to show you how much I admire you for your leadership.

KING: How pleased I am! I must look again at those beautiful horses. Come, my Queen, you must see them before deciding upon a reward. . . . Such a fine lot of animals!

QUEEN: These fine horses must have cost a fortune. Just

166

see how proudly they hold their heads!

KING: Now what shall we give the rich man?

NARRATOR: The Queen and King talk quietly. The Queen speaks.

QUEEN: It is what he deserves!

KING: Of course. The very thing! How clever you are! My friend, you shall have as a reward the most wonderful thing in our palace! Only this morning a farmer brought us the most wonderful turnip in the world. It is so large that it will hardly fit into a cart and had to be pulled by two horses. In return we gave her a bag of gold and jewels!

RICH BROTHER: (*Eagerly*) Yes, yes, Your Majesty.

KING: You shall have this turnip.

RICH BROTHER: Thank you, Your . . . a turnip! You mean. . . .

KING: Yes, I mean that you shall have this wonderful vegetable.

RICH BROTHER: But . . . Your Majesty . . . I. . . .

KING: Say no more, my good fellow! Such a generous gift as yours is indeed worthy of the most wonderful thing in the whole kingdom.

RICH BROTHER: But, Your Highness, I sold all of my possessions and spent all of my money . . .

167

KING: . . . to bring us a present. Indeed, you are the only one to receive this most unusual reward! Guards, take him out and give him this wonderful turnip. He shall have the cart and horses as well.

RICH BROTHER: (*Protesting*) But, Your Majesty, please listen to me. I tell you that I . . .

KING: . . . have never seen anything as wonderful! Neither have we. And you are the only one to whom we would give it.

RICH BROTHER: (*In despair*) I'm ruined! Yes, guards, I'm coming.

KING: My dear Queen, how clever of you to think of giving our dear friend what he deserves!

Focus

1. How did the Queen learn of the rich brother's plan?
2. The rich brother gave the Queen and King horses as a gift. Why?
3. What was the rich brother's reward and why did he receive it?
4. Tell why the rich brother's reward was or was not a good one.
5. In a play, how do you know what the characters are feeling?

SOCIAL STUDIES READING: What's It All About?

The country in the play you just read was ruled by a king and queen. Once, queens and kings were the leaders of many countries and cities. Today many different people rule, or govern, countries and cities. You can read about government in a social studies book. Here are some hints to help you with your social studies reading.

TAKE A FIRST LOOK

Look at the social studies page printed here. What is the title on this page? What does it tell you this page is about?

FIND THE KEY IDEAS

Look through the words on the next page. Do you see one in special *slanted* letters? (Letters like these are called italics.) This is an important word. Read the sentence the word is in. What does it hint that *citizens* means?

READ CAREFULLY

Now read the whole page carefully. Who is in charge of running the city of San Francisco? What workers are needed to help the mayor run the city? You may want to read the page two times. That way, you will be sure to understand how to use the page.

CITY GOVERNMENT IN SAN FRANCISCO

People who live together in a city are its *citizens.* They work to make the city a good place in which to live. They vote to choose people to run the city.

In San Francisco the mayor is in charge of running the city. The citizens elect the mayor. On election day the citizens also choose some of the mayor's helpers.

Many workers are needed to help the mayor run the city. Some keep the streets and the parks clean. Fire fighters, police officers, and health inspectors help keep citizens safe. People who work in public libraries work for the city. People who work in public schools and city hospitals work for the city.

The money to pay all of these people comes from taxes. People who live in the city pay taxes. Businesses pay taxes, too. Everyone who lives in the city helps pay to run the city.

Who are the government workers in your city or town? What work do they do?

171

Some get turnips, some get. . . . What does Rhinoceros get?

How the Rhinoceros Kept His Skin

Clare T. Read

A long time ago there was a Parsee who lived way up in the highest of mountains. He was very, very old and very, very wise. He could see things that could almost never be seen. He could hear things that could almost never be heard. Everyone came to him for advice and favors.

One day Rhinoceros went to the Parsee to ask an important favor. He wanted a new skin because

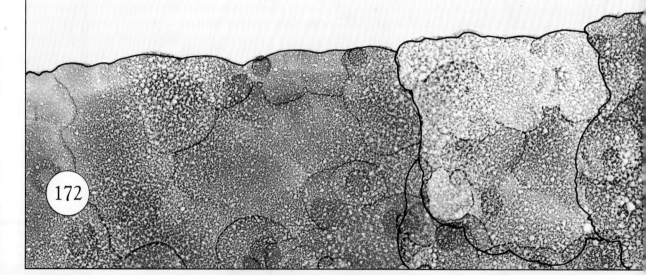

he thought his skin looked ugly. All the animals laughed at him. So he walked up to the Parsee. Using his best manners, he asked, "Oh Parsee, could you do me a great favor?"

The Parsee smiled at Rhinoceros and said only, "I *could* do you a favor if only I *would* do you a favor."

Rhinoceros looked puzzled. But he went on, again using his best manners, "Oh *wonderful* Parsee, I would like a new skin. The one I have now is ugly. It is all tough, wrinkled, and scratched. If only you would give me a smooth and silky skin, I would be a most happy rhinoceros."

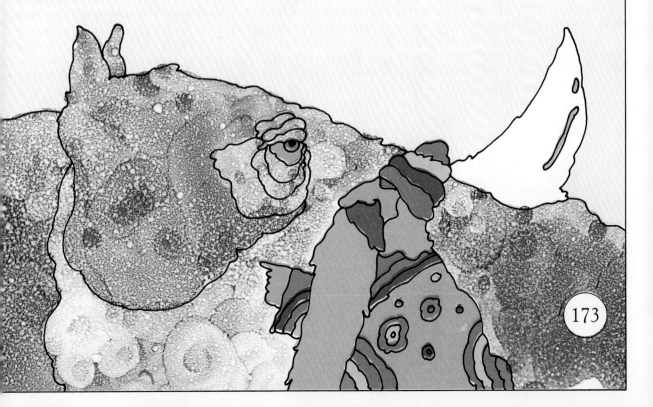

The Parsee frowned and said, "You are the way you are because that is the way you *should* be."

Again Rhinoceros was confused. He wasn't sure what the Parsee was thinking. He decided to try one last time. Once more he used his best manners.

"Oh *greatest* Parsee, please give me a new skin," he asked. "All the other animals laugh at me."

The Parsee stared at Rhinoceros for a long time. He scratched his chin. Rhinoceros hoped the Parsee would be kind and grant him the favor of a new skin. Finally the Parsee spoke.

"If you would be something that you are not, you may be sorry. Are you sure your favor should be granted?"

"Yes, yes, yes!" said Rhinoceros.

The Parsee raised his hands above him and chanted:

Let it be so,
Though he may woe.
May the skin with the folds
Look silky and bold.
Now go!

Rhinoceros looked down and saw his new skin. It was smooth and silky. The sun's rays made it glimmer.

"Hooray!" he shouted. "I have a new skin. We'll see what the animals have to say now."

Rhinoceros then started merrily down the mountain singing the Parsee's chant to himself. He wasn't quite sure what the second line meant, but he sang it anyway.

Rhinoceros came home, marching with his head and shoulders held high. He thought that he was handsome now! But when he passed Camel and Baboon he heard them whisper, "Who's that? He looks like an over-sized pig with a horn." They laughed loudly.

Then he passed Tiger and Zebra and heard them whisper, "Who does Rhinoceros think he is? Now everyone will laugh at the animal kingdom for having a rhinoceros that looks like a hippo. He should be ashamed of himself."

This was not at all what Rhinoceros had expected. He went home with his head and shoulders hung low. He was sad, tired, and hungry after his long trip. When he got home to his palm tree he had his favorite supper—bread.

Now, Rhinoceros loved bread. In fact,

sometimes he ate only bread for weeks and weeks. Of course, there were bread crumbs all around his palm tree.

After supper Rhinoceros lay down to sleep. But he had a terrible time getting to sleep. The bread crumbs made his bed very uncomfortable. Before, with his old, tough skin, he never even felt the crumbs. Now that his skin was smooth, Rhinoceros felt every little crumb.

All night he rolled and rolled trying to get rid of the itch. All night he scratched and scratched. Finally, he got up in the darkness and rubbed against his palm tree.

"Ah, that feels good," Rhinoceros said to himself. He rubbed and rubbed and rubbed. Soon he became very tired. Finally he fell asleep leaning against his palm tree.

The next morning he headed down to the river for a bath. On the way he passed Camel and Baboon. He heard them say, "Look! Rhinoceros looks much better this morning. At least we will know who he is."

Rhinoceros was pleased when he heard that. Then he passed Tiger and Zebra. "Well," said Tiger, "Rhinoceros will not be a disgrace to us now, thank goodness." Rhinoceros was now *very* happy. His new skin was a success!

When he came to the river he was about to plunge in when he saw himself in the water. He gasped when he saw that his new smooth and silky skin was now all rough and scratchy, with great folds over his shoulders.

He was about to cry out when he remembered what the animals had said. He remembered, too, what the Parsee had said about being the way he *should* be. After remembering for a while he forgot about crying and just smiled to himself. He took his

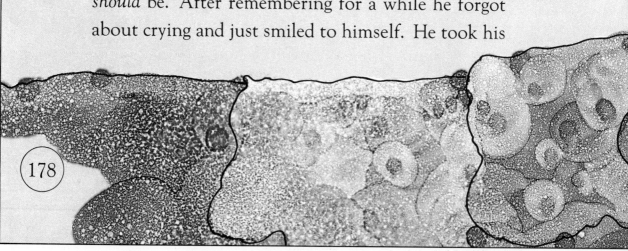

bath and trotted home to his favorite palm tree, humming the Parsee's chant.

To this day Rhinoceros has been content with his rough and scratchy skin. He knows now what the Parsee meant by the second line of the chant. He knows that he is just the way he *should* be.

Focus

1. What did Rhinoceros want, and why did he think the Parsee could help him?
2. Why was the Parsee's chant important?
3. Why was Rhinoceros happy at the end?

Rhino Jokes

Why do rhinos paint their toenails red? (So they can hide in cherry trees.)

Why can't you see rhinos hiding in cherry trees? (Because rhinos paint their toenails red.)

Why do rhinos wear blue sneakers? (So they can hide in a blueberry patch.)

Why do rhinos wear sneakers? (So you won't hear them when they jump out of trees.)

Why do rhinos wear green sneakers? (So they can walk across the grass without being seen.)

Why do rhinos wear ripple-soled sneakers? (To give the ants a fair chance.)

How would you get five rhinos in a car? (Two in the front seat, two in the back seat, and one in the glove compartment.)

Why do rhinos float on their backs? (To keep their sneakers dry.)

How would you get four giraffes in the car? (You couldn't—it's full of rhinos.)

What's gray and goes "slam, slam, slam, slam?" (A four-door rhino.)

181

The story about the rhinoceros is made up. What stories about animals are true?

Animal Fact/ Animal Fable
Seymour Simon

Raccoons Wash Their Food.
Fact or Fiction?

Raccoons often dip their food in water. But they are not washing it. They are making it easier to eat.

A raccoon's throat is not very large. Raccoons have trouble eating large pieces of food. Dipping food in water makes it easier to swallow. When raccoons find a mushy piece of fruit, they don't wash the food. They just gulp it down right away.

Elephants Are Afraid of Mice.
Fact or Fiction?

We often see mice in elephant stalls in zoos. At times the mice come very close to an elephant's trunk. Some people think the big animals are afraid the mice will run up their trunks. But the elephants don't seem to mind.

If a mouse did run up an elephant's trunk, it wouldn't hurt.

The elephant would just blow out the mouse with one good sneeze.

Cats Have Nine Lives.
Fact or Fiction?

Since early times, people have said that cats have nine lives. Cats are very quick and clever. But cats, like all animals, have only one life to lose.

Many animals can hurt themselves if they fall from a height. But cats are so nimble that they often land on their feet and walk away. Cats jump and move so easily that it seems as if they are never hurt. Of course, that's not so. Cats do get hurt.

Some Fish Climb Trees.
Fact or Fiction?

Most fish can't climb trees, but the mud skipper can. Skippers climb up logs or the branches of trees that lean into the water. Even when out of the water, skippers can breathe air through their gills.

The mud skipper lives in many parts of the world. It looks like a mixture of a fish, a tadpole, and a frog. Skippers use their thick front fins to skip about on the land. They are looking for insects and other things to eat.

Focus

1. Why does a raccoon seem to wash its food before it eats?
2. What would an elephant do if a mouse ran up its trunk?
3. Explain why people say that cats have nine lives.
4. What does a mud skipper look like?

Sometimes storytellers try to tell more than just a story. What else do you think Aesop is trying to tell you in this fable?

The Fox and the Stork

Fox liked a good laugh. And he especially liked to laugh at Stork, who he thought was an odd-looking creature.

Now, one day Fox invited Stork to dinner.

"We'll have a few good chuckles," he promised.

But Stork didn't have a good chuckle. For when she arrived, Fox served her soup in a plate. Stork couldn't even taste it. She could only wet the tip of her bill.

As for Fox, he lapped up his soup, chuckling. "Laugh!" he said. "It's a joke!"

But Stork didn't laugh. Instead she said, "Come to my home for dinner tomorrow."

The next day Fox went to Stork's house. And what did Stork do but serve him a wonderful-smelling stew. But she served it in a tall, narrow-necked jar. Hungry Fox couldn't even get his nose into that narrow-necked jar.

"One good laugh deserves another!" laughed Stork. She ate up her own stew and Fox's as well.

Aesop says: Treat others as you would like them to treat you.

Focus

1. How did Fox serve Stork dinner? What was Stork's problem?
2. Stork served Fox stew in a narrow-necked jar. Why?
3. What did Fox and you learn from Aesop?
4. In a fable, what is the author trying to do?

187

**Vocabulary:
Word
Identification**

On your paper complete each sentence with one of the words on the right. You will have one word left over.

1. Walking behind someone is called _____.
2. An animal with a horn is a _____.
3. A person who lives next door is a _____.
4. Something strange is _____.
5. Something that is not a fact is _____.

neighbor

unusual

rhinoceros

fiction

following

manners

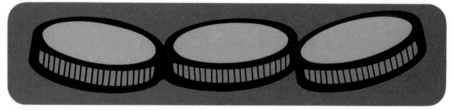

**Vocabulary:
Vocabulary
Development
(multiple
meanings)**

Choose words from the right that make sense in each sentence. On your paper write the complete sentences. Use each word twice.

6. I will help you in one _____.
7. You used to be in the _____ grade.
8. Luis was _____ when the toy broke.
9. The players wanted to _____ the rules.
10. The race will _____ here, so take your places.
11. Anna was surprised and turned with a _____.
12. The clerk gave Maria _____ for her dollar.
13. The traffic guard let the children _____ the road.

start

cross

second

change

Read the story below. Think of what might happen next. Comprehension: Predicting Outcomes

One day a man was walking along a road. He had on a heavy coat because the wind was blowing hard. He held the coat close. Then the sun came out and shone brightly. Even though the wind was still blowing, the man was getting hotter and hotter.

14. On your paper write this sentence and finish it with one of the phrases below: In a little while the man . . .

a. ran away.   b. took off his coat.

c. put on another coat.   d. sang and danced.

Read each sentence. Then write each sentence on your paper filling in the blanks with the words on the right. One word will be left over. Decoding: Consonants *lk, mb*

15. The rhinoceros found that
bread _____ can be itchy.   stalk

16. The tree _____ broke in the storm.   limb

17. Use a _____ to make your hair neat.   comb

18. Elephants swing their trunks as they _____.   crumbs

19. Cats like to _____ mice.   walk

chalk

189

A violent rainstorm left the creek gushing and angry. By the time Laura thought about playing with danger it was almost too late. Would something terrible happen?

The Footbridge

Laura Ingalls Wilder

Next day Laura was sure that Ma would not let her go to play in the creek. It was roaring, but more softly than the day before. In the dugout she could hear it calling her. So Laura quietly slipped outdoors without saying anything to Ma.

The water was not so high now. It had gone down from the steps and Laura could see it foaming against the footbridge. Part of the plank was above the water.

All winter the creek had been covered with ice; it had been motionless and still, never making a sound. Now it was running swiftly and making a joyful noise. Where it struck the edge of the plank, it foamed up in white bubbles and laughed to itself.

191

Laura took off her shoes and stockings and put them safely on the bottom step. Then she walked out on the plank and stood watching the noisy water.

Drops splashed her bare feet and thin little waves ran around them. She dabbled one foot in the swirling foam. Then down she sat on the plank and plumped both legs into the water. The creek ran strong against them and she kicked against it. That was fun!

Now she was wet almost all over, but her whole skin wanted to be in the water. She lay on her stomach and thrust her arms down on each side of the plank, deep into the fast current. But that was not enough. She wanted to be really in the roaring, joyous creek. She clasped her hands together under the plank and rolled off it.

In that very instant, she knew the creek was not playing. It was strong and terrible. It seized her whole body and pulled it under the plank. Only her head was out, and one arm was thrown desperately across the narrow plank.

The water was pulling her, and it was pushing, too. It was trying to drag her head under the plank. Her chin held onto the edge and her arm clutched, while the water pulled hard at all the rest of her. It was not laughing now.

No one knew where she was. No one could hear her if she screamed for help. The water roared loud and tugged at her, stronger and stronger. Laura kicked, but the water was stronger than her legs.

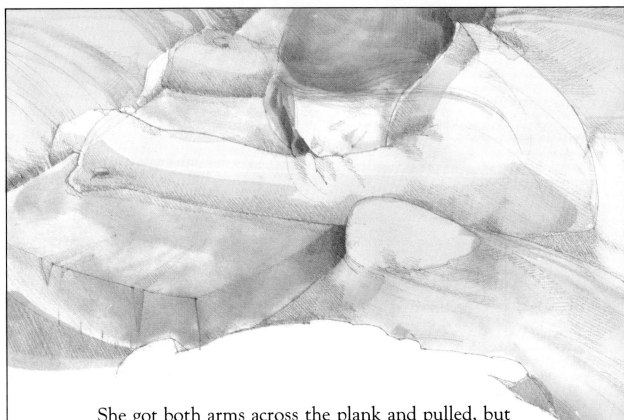

She got both arms across the plank and pulled, but the water pulled harder. It pulled the back of her head down and it jerked as if it would jerk her in two. It was cold. The coldness soaked into her.

This was not like wolves or cattle. The creek was not alive. It was only strong and terrible and never stopping. It would pull her down and whirl her away, rolling and tossing her like a willow branch. It would not care.

Her legs were tired, and her arms hardly felt the plank any more.

"I must get out. I must!" she thought. The creek's roaring was in her head. She kicked hard with both her feet and pulled hard with her arms, and then she was lying on the plank again.

The plank was solid under her stomach and under her face. She lay on it and breathed and was glad it was solid.

When she moved, her head whirled. She crawled off the plank. She took her shoes and her stockings and she climbed slowly up the muddy steps. At the door of the dugout she stopped. She did not know what to say to Ma.

After a while she went in. Just inside the door she stood still and water dripped off her. Ma was sewing.

"Where have you been, Laura?" Ma asked, looking up. Then she came quickly, saying: "My goodness! Turn around, quick!" She began unbuttoning Laura down the back. "What happened? Did you fall in the creek?"

"No, ma'am," Laura said. "I—I went in."

Ma listened and went on undressing Laura and rubbing her hard all over with a towel. She did not say a word even when Laura had told her everything. Laura's teeth chattered, and Ma wrapped a quilt around her and sat her close to the stove.

At last Ma said: "Well, Laura, you have been very naughty, and I think you knew it all the time. But I can't punish you. I can't even scold you. You came near being drowned."

Laura did not say anything.

"You won't go near the creek again till Pa or I say you may, and that won't be till the water goes down," said Ma.

"No'm," Laura said.

The creek would go down. It would be a gentle, pleasant place to play in again. But nobody could make it do that. Nobody could make it do anything. Laura knew now that there were things stronger than anybody. But the creek had not got her. It had not made her scream and it could not make her cry.

Focus

1. Laura did not tell her mother where she was going to play. Why not?
2. Why didn't Laura call for help when she fell into the creek?
3. How did Laura save herself?
4. Why didn't Laura's mother punish her?
5. Laura was not afraid of the creek. Why not?

197

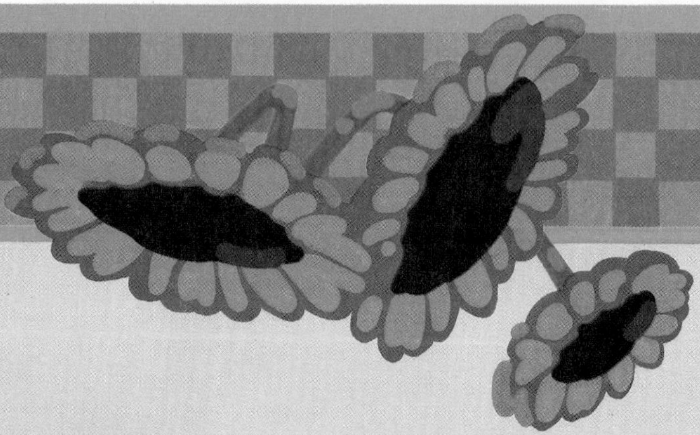

Change

The summer
still hangs
heavy and sweet
with sunlight
as it did last year.

The autumn
still comes
showering gold and crimson
as it did last year.

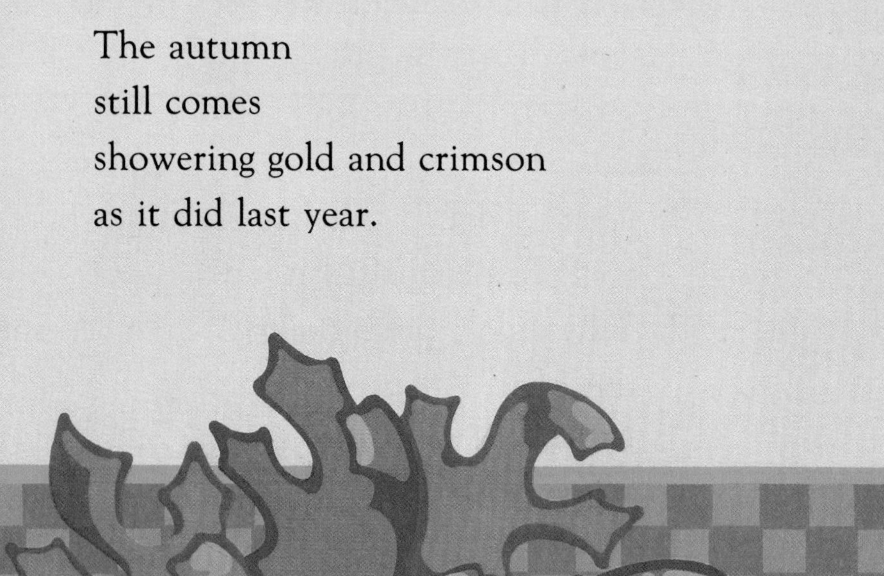

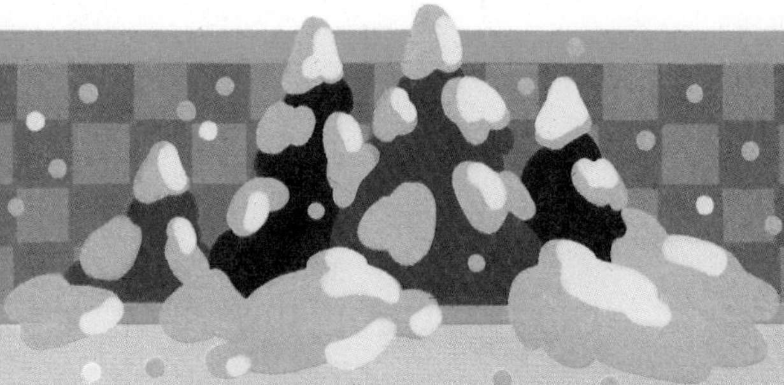

The winter
still stings
clean and cold and white
as it did last year.

The spring
still comes
like a whisper in the dark night.
It is only I
who have changed.

Charlotte Zolotow

Young and daring Laura had quite an adventure at the footbridge. The life of the author, Laura Ingalls Wilder, was exciting, too.

Laura Ingalls Wilder, Storyteller

Peggy Warner

Think for a minute about where you now live. Now take away roads, telephones, cars, trains, and planes. Take away all your neighbors. Take away supermarkets. Take away zoos. You and your family are all by yourselves. You will build your own house. You will grow your own food.

It is hard to know what our country was like not too long ago. Laura Ingalls Wilder knew. She had crossed the plains with her family in a covered wagon. She knew what it was like to be a child in the 1800s. And she wrote it all down in books. She wrote these books to tell children about life in early

America. Laura once said, "I wanted the children to know more about the start of things . . . what it was that made America."

You might know Laura's most famous book. It's called *Little House on the Prairie*. It was written more than fifty years ago. It was her best-loved book, and the story became a popular TV show.

Laura Ingalls Wilder was born in a log cabin in Wisconsin early in 1867. When Laura was small, her family moved across the plains in a covered wagon. Many families moved like this. Land was free so long as a family lived on it. Some land did not make a good farm. Families then looked for better land.

On the grassy prairies there was often no wood to build a house. But there was lots and lots of grass. Farmers dug up strips of sod and made houses of them. Sometimes flowers grew on the roof. Laura once lived in one of these houses.

The Ingalls family finally moved across the plains to Minnesota where they had a farm. Life was often hard. There were floods and blizzards. Wild animals ate the crops. The Ingalls family had to be strong.

"Ma taught us how to read and trained us in our manners," Laura wrote later. "Pa taught us other things and told us stories." Life was different in those days. "There was no radio," Laura said. "We had no movies to go see. When the day's work was done, we sat in the twilight. We listened to Pa's stories or to the music of his fiddle."

When the Ingalls family left the farm, they moved to a little town in South Dakota. There Laura grew from a child to a young woman. When she was 15, she taught school. Three years later she married a farmer, Almanzo Wilder. Those were happy years. One of their joys was their child, Rose.

There were hard times, too. There was sickness, and hailstones ruined the crops one year. Laura and Almanzo lost their farm. Still the Wilders kept their dream. They had always wanted to go to Missouri to live. So they saved their money, and after a few years Laura and Almanzo had enough to move.

The trip to Missouri took a long time. Missouri was more than six hundred miles away, and the Wilders went there by horse and wagon. As they traveled the long miles to their new home, they met many people. Laura kept a diary about the people they met. In the diary she wrote of the towns they saw and the things that happened. At last they reached Missouri, and the Wilders felt that they were finally home.

The Wilders loved Missouri. At first they lived in a tiny log cabin. Year by year they added to their home. They planted an orchard. They raised hogs and sheep, cattle, and goats. They made many friends, too.

Their daughter Rose grew up and moved away. One day Rose wrote her mother a letter. Rose asked her mother to write down the stories she had told Rose as a child. Laura liked the idea and took out her old diary.

"Children today could not have a childhood like mine," she thought. "But they could learn of it and hear the stories Pa used to tell."

Laura's first book was called *Little House in the Big Woods*. Children begged her to write more. So Laura wrote seven more books. One of these was *On the Banks of Plum Creek* that tells the story "The Footbridge." The favorite of almost everyone is *Little House on the Prairie*. Laura Ingalls Wilder's books won many prizes. She is known as one of early America's best storytellers.

Focus

1. Where did Laura grow up?
2. Where did the Wilders finally settle?
3. Who first asked Laura to write stories? Why did Laura agree to begin writing?
4. Where did she get her ideas for her stories?
5. Where do you think storytellers sometimes get ideas for their stories?

STUDY SKILL: Table of Contents

"The Footbridge" by Laura Ingalls Wilder is just one chapter from the book *On the Banks of Plum Creek*. To find out what some of the other chapters are, you would look in the table of contents.

A table of contents is at the beginning of most books. It lists the parts of a book in order from beginning to end. A table of contents tells you these things:

1. The titles of the chapters in the book
2. The page on which each chapter begins

Contents

 CONTENTS

What do you know about a table of contents? Answer these questions on a sheet of paper.

1. Where in a book can you find the table of contents?
2. List two things a table of contents tells you.
3. Look at the table of contents on this page. What is the title of Chapter 5? On what page does it begin?
4. From the titles of the chapters what would you expect the book to be about?

Laura Ingalls Wilder wrote stories about real-life adventures. Say "hello" to A. A. Milne's make-believe friends in the adventures of Edward Bear.

Winnie-the-Pooh

A. A. Milne

Edward Bear, known to his friends as Winnie-the-Pooh, or Pooh for short, was walking through the forest one day, humming proudly to himself. He had made up a little hum that very morning, as he was doing his Stoutness Exercises in front of the glass: Tra-la-la, tra-la-la, as he stretched up as high as he could go, and then Tra-la-la, tra-la—oh, help!—la, as he tried to reach his toes. After breakfast he had said it over and over to himself until he had learnt it off by heart, and now he was humming it right through, properly. It went like this:

Tra-la-la, tra-la-la,
Tra-la-la, tra-la-la,
Rum-tum-tiddle-um-tum.
Tiddle-iddle, tiddle-iddle,
Tiddle-iddle, tiddle-iddle,
Rum-tum-tum-tiddle-um.

Well, he was humming this hum to himself, and walking along gaily, wondering what everybody else was doing, and what it felt like, being somebody else, when suddenly he came to a sandy bank, and in the bank was a large hole.

"Aha!" said Pooh. (Rum-tum-tiddle-um-tum.) "If I know anything about anything, that hole means Rabbit," he said, "and Rabbit means Company," he said, "and company means Food and Listening-to-Me-Humming and such like. Rum-tum-tum-tiddle-um."

So he bent down, put his head into the hole, and called out:

"Is anybody at home?"

There was a sudden scuffling noise from inside the hole, and then silence.

"What I said was, 'Is anybody at home?'" called out Pooh very loudly.

"No!" said a voice; and then added, "you needn't shout so loud. I heard you quite well the first time."

"Bother!" said Pooh. "Isn't there anybody here at all?"

"Nobody."

innie-the-Pooh took his head out of the hole, and thought for a little, and he thought to himself, "There must be somebody there, because somebody must have said 'Nobody.'" So he put his head back in the hole, and said:

"Hallo, Rabbit, isn't that you?"

"No," said Rabbit, in a different sort of voice this time.

"But isn't that Rabbit's voice?"

"I don't think so," said Rabbit. "It isn't meant to be."

"Oh!" said Pooh.

He took his head out of the hole, and had another think, and then he put it back, and said:

"Well, could you very kindly tell me where Rabbit is?"

"He has gone to see his friend Pooh Bear, who is a great friend of his."

"But this is Me!" said Bear, very much surprised.

"What sort of Me?"

"Pooh Bear."

"Are you sure?" said Rabbit, still more surprised.

"Quite, quite sure," said Pooh.

"Oh, well, then, come in."

So Pooh pushed and pushed and pushed his way through the hole, and at last he got in.

"You were quite right," said Rabbit, looking at him all over. "It is you. Glad to see you."

"Who did you think it was?"

"Well, I wasn't sure. You know how it is in the Forest. One can't have anybody coming into one's house. One has to be careful. What about a mouthful of something?"

Pooh always liked a little something at eleven o'clock in the morning, and he was very glad to see Rabbit getting out the plates and mugs; and when Rabbit said, "Honey or condensed milk with your bread?" he was so excited that he said, "Both," and then, so as not to seem greedy, he added, "But don't bother about the bread, please." And for a long time after that he said nothing . . . until at last, humming at himself in a rather sticky voice, he got up, shook Rabbit lovingly by the paw, and said that he must be going on.

"Must you?" said Rabbit politely.

"Well," said Pooh, "I could stay a little longer if it—if you—" and he tried very hard to look in the direction of the larder.

"As a matter of fact," said Rabbit, "I was going out myself directly."

"Oh, well, then, I'll be going on. Good-bye."

"Well, good-bye, if you're sure you won't have any more."

"Is there any more?" asked Pooh quickly.

Rabbit took the covers off the dishes, and said, "No, there wasn't."

"I thought not," said Pooh, nodding to himself. "Well, good-bye. I must be going on."

So he started to climb out of the hole. He pulled with his front paws, and pushed with his back paws, and in a little while his nose was out in

the open again . . . and then his ears . . . and then his front paws . . . and then his shoulders . . . and then—

"Oh, help!" said Pooh. "I'd better go back."

"Oh, bother!" said Pooh. "I shall have to go on."

"I can't do either!" said Pooh. "Oh, help and bother!"

ow by this time Rabbit wanted to go for a walk too, and finding the front door full, he went out by the back door, and came round to Pooh, and looked at him.

"Hallo, are you stuck?" he asked.

"No—no," said Pooh carelessly. "Just resting and thinking and humming to myself."

"Here, give us a paw."

Pooh Bear stretched out a paw, and Rabbit pulled and pulled and pulled. . . .

"Ow!" cried Pooh. "You're hurting!"

"The fact is," said Rabbit, "you're stuck."

"It all comes," said Pooh crossly, "of not having front doors big enough."

"It all comes," said Rabbit sternly, "of eating

too much. I thought at the time," said Rabbit, "only I didn't like to say anything," said Rabbit, "that one of us was eating too much," said Rabbit, "and I knew it wasn't me," he said. "Well, well, I shall go and fetch Christopher Robin."

Christopher Robin lived at the other end of the Forest, and when he came back with Rabbit, and saw the front half of Pooh, he said, "Silly old Bear," in such a loving voice that everybody felt quite hopeful again.

"I was just beginning to think," said Bear, sniffing slightly, "that Rabbit might never be able to use his front door again. And I should hate that," he said.

"So should I," said Rabbit.

"Use his front door again?" said Christopher Robin. "Of course he'll use his front door again."

"Good," said Rabbit.

"If we can't pull you out, Pooh, we might push you back."

Rabbit scratched his whiskers thoughtfully, and pointed out that, when once Pooh was pushed back, he was back, and of course nobody was more glad to see Pooh than he was, still there it was, some lived in trees and some lived underground, and—

"You mean I'd never get out?" said Pooh.

"I mean," said Rabbit, "that having got so far, it seems a pity to waste it."

Christopher Robin nodded.

"Then there's only one thing to be done," he said. "We shall have to wait for you to get thin again."

"How long does getting thin take?" asked Pooh anxiously.

"About a week, I should think."

"But I can't stay here for a week!"

"You can stay here all right, silly old Bear. It's getting you out which is so difficult."

"We'll read to you," said Rabbit cheerfully.

"And I hope it won't snow," he added. "And I say, old fellow, you're taking up a good deal of room in my house . . . do you mind if I use your back legs as a towel-horse? Because, I mean, there they are . . . doing nothing . . . and it would be very convenient just to hang the towels on them."

"A week!" said Pooh gloomily. "What about meals?"

"I'm afraid no meals," said Christopher Robin, "because of getting thin quicker. But we will read to you."

Bear began to sigh, and then found he couldn't because he was so tightly stuck; and a tear rolled down his eye, as he said:

"Then would you read a Sustaining Book, such as would help and comfort a Wedged Bear in Great Tightness?"

So for a week Christopher Robin read that sort of book at the North end of Pooh, and Rabbit hung his washing on the South end . . . and in between Bear felt himself getting slenderer and slenderer. And at the end of the week Christopher Robin said, "Now!"

So he took hold of Pooh's front paws and Rabbit took hold of Christopher Robin, and all

Rabbit's friends and relations took hold of Rabbit, and they all pulled together. . . .

And for a long time Pooh only said "Ow!" . . .

And "Oh!" . . .

And then, all of a sudden, he said "Pop!" just as if a cork were coming out of a bottle.

And Christopher Robin and Rabbit and all Rabbit's friends and relations went head-over-heels backwards . . . and on the top of them came Winnie-the-Pooh—free!

So, with a nod of thanks to his friends, he went on with his walk through the forest, humming

proudly to himself. But Christopher Robin looked after him lovingly, and said to himself, "Silly old Bear!"

Focus

1. Why did Pooh want to visit Rabbit?
2. Rabbit did not welcome Pooh into his home right away. Why not?
3. Why did Pooh finally decide to leave Rabbit's house?
4. What reason did Pooh give for getting stuck in Rabbit's door?
   What reason did Rabbit give? Who was right? Explain why.
5. How did Pooh finally get free?
6. Christopher Robin called Pooh a "silly old bear." Do you agree? Tell why or why not.

CHECKPOINT

Read these sentences and the words under each. On your paper write each sentence with the word that fits in it.

1. Laura once lived on the _____.

polite   proper   plains

2. The sun comes up _____ in the morning.

terrible   early   diary

3. _____ is a large place.

Almanzo   Christopher   America

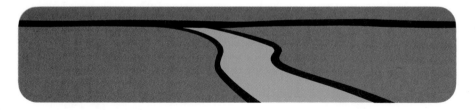

Read the paragraph below. What will happen next?

Pooh's house was near a stream. The stream looked cool that hot day. Pooh stood by the water's edge. He stuck his toe in the water to test how cold it was. Then he . . .

4. On your paper write "Then he" and finish the sentence with one of the phrases below:

    a. visited Christopher Robin.

    b. ate his lunch.

    c. went wading.

Use one of these words to answer each question below. Decoding: Consonants *lk, mb*
Write the answer on your paper.

chalk   lamb   talk   yolk   folk

5. What do you use to write on a board?

6. What is the yellow part of an egg called?

7. What animal gives us wool?

8. What do people do when they speak?

Look at the table of contents below. Then on your paper Study Skills: Book Parts (table of contents)
answer the questions that follow.

Contents	Page
I. In Which We Are Introduced to Winnie-the-Pooh and Some Bees, and the Stories Begin	3
II. In Which Pooh Goes Visiting and Gets Into a Tight Place	22
III. In Which Pooh and Piglet Go Hunting and Nearly Catch a Woozle	34

9. On what page would you find a story about Piglet?

10. What is the title of Chapter II?

11. What story would you find on page 3?

Sending

People are full of jabber, doodle, and wigwag. We talk. We draw. We move. It's all called communication. Some people like to talk or sing. Some paint, take pictures, or write, and, of course, musicians play. Think about dancing. It lets you send messages without speaking one word.

Come with the people in this unit. A photographer will say a lot with her camera. You'll find out how to make music with drinking glasses. Then join a little band in a big parade. Next, discover "moving" ways to communicate. Get ready to go off on an adventure with a secret club called . . . well, that's a secret.

First, jabber, doodle, and wigwag with Alvin. He'd like to show you his "masterpiece."

222

Messages

Alvin thinks he's a fantastic doodler. What do you think of his "work of art"?

Alvin's Masterpiece

John H. Noble

Alvin Artwork just loved to paint. I suppose it had to do with his last name. He had a strange way of painting, though. Splat! The paint would fly onto his art paper. Splosh! The paint would fly onto his shirt. Splish! The paint would splatter all over his pants. Squish! By mistake he'd sit down on his purple paint dish.

One day Alvin was working on his masterpiece. The paint was everywhere! Somehow, he managed to keep the paint inside his studio. It was just about everywhere else, though. But oh, what a painting he was painting! Every now and then he stepped back and took a long look at what he had done so far. "Oh," he said. "Ah," he sighed. "My oh my! This is my best," he said, patting himself on the back.

Alvin kept painting for the rest of the morning. But the more he painted, the more he worried. The painting wasn't getting any better. It had been much better before, when he had said, "Oh," "ah," and "my oh my." He was very discouraged. What could he do? It would be very hard to take paint off the paper. "Hmmm," he said to himself. He walked

around the room, stroking his chin with his painty fingers.

He happened to pass his large boy-sized mirror as he was pacing about. He was still deep in thought about what to do. He gave an off-hand look into the mirror. Suddenly, his face lit up!

"I have it!" he cried. "The masterpiece is right in front of me. It's fantastic! I'm beautiful!" He looked carefully into the mirror. He *was* beautiful! The paint covered him from head to toe in an amazing splash of color. The reds were brilliant. The yellows were sunny. The greens were grassy, and the oranges were so orangey you could almost taste them. This was not to mention the pinks that were shocking and the blues that were beautiful!

But Alvin sighed. "How will I show this masterpiece to everyone? I can't take my clothes off to show it . . . that would ruin it. I must think of something." Alvin thought hard while he looked at

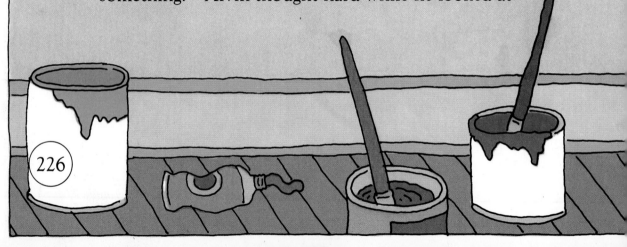

himself in the mirror. Finally Alvin had a very good idea, and he began to work on it.

In the corner of the studio, he found his tool box hidden under his smock. Then, he searched for some scraps of wood that he knew were around somewhere. He found some nails in an old, empty can of blue paint. So, he started hammering away. In no time at all he had a perfect Alvin-sized picture frame. He held it up in front of him and looked into the mirror. It was wonderful!

"Now what?" he asked himself. "To the museum," he answered. Before he started on his way he took an almost-clean piece of paper and carefully printed:

THE MASTERPIECE BY ALVIN ARTWORK

He stuck the paper on his picture frame and started out the door of his studio. He went down the stairs and across the street to the Museum of Modern Art.

Alvin went in the back door of the museum without anyone seeing him. He found a comfortable place to stand. Then Alvin leaned up against the wall. He held the picture frame very straight. Soon people began coming around. They all looked at him.

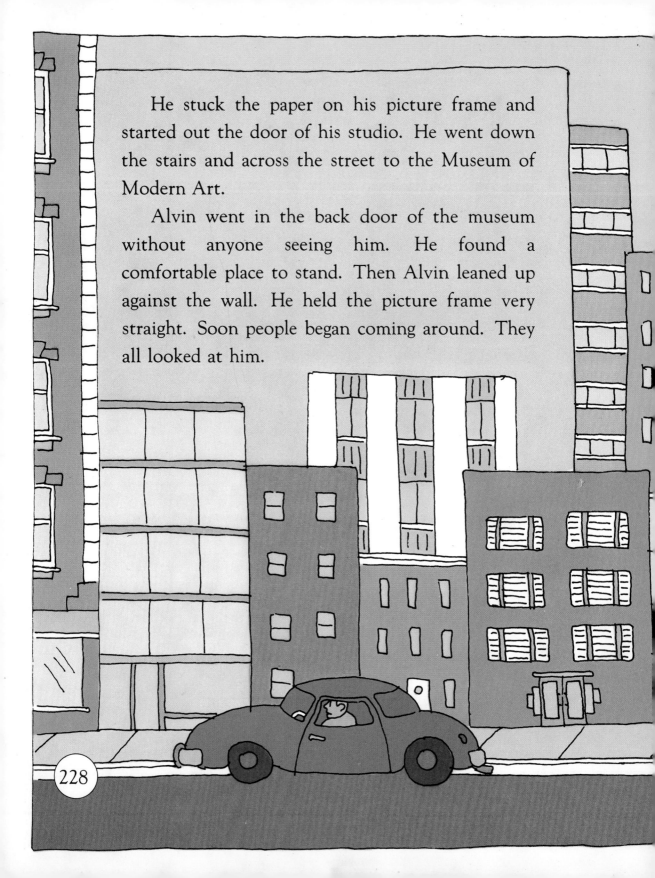

"Oh," they said, "what a work of art!"

"Ah," they said, "this is a masterpiece." The people stared at him for a long time. They seemed to like Alvin's painting a lot. In fact, he heard them say, "Let's go get the others. They should see this." They left chattering away about the masterpiece they had just seen.

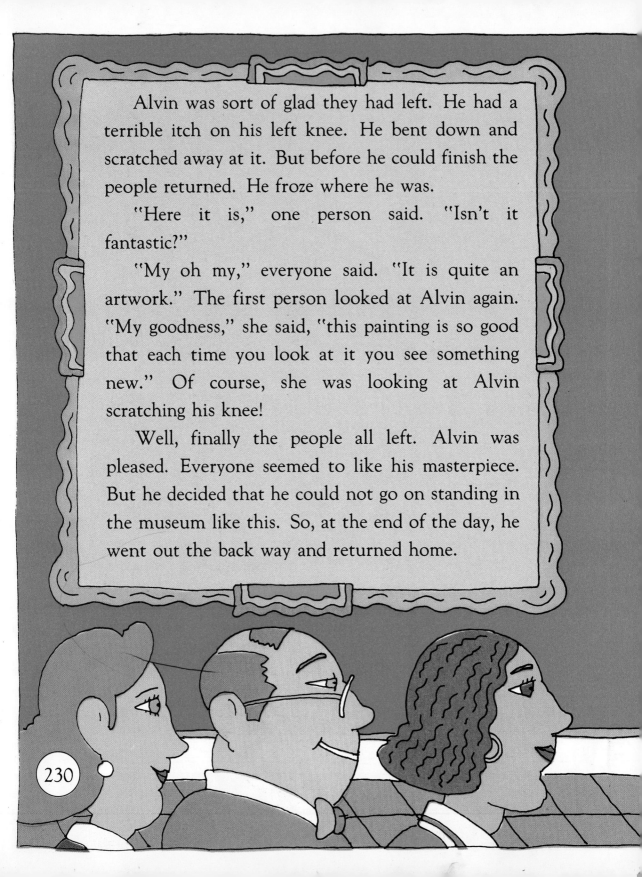

Alvin was sort of glad they had left. He had a terrible itch on his left knee. He bent down and scratched away at it. But before he could finish the people returned. He froze where he was.

"Here it is," one person said. "Isn't it fantastic?"

"My oh my," everyone said. "It is quite an artwork." The first person looked at Alvin again. "My goodness," she said, "this painting is so good that each time you look at it you see something new." Of course, she was looking at Alvin scratching his knee!

Well, finally the people all left. Alvin was pleased. Everyone seemed to like his masterpiece. But he decided that he could not go on standing in the museum like this. So, at the end of the day, he went out the back way and returned home.

Painting a masterpiece was hard work, and he needed rest. He didn't mind having to ruin his work of art when it was time for bed. Now he knew that he could paint a masterpiece. But the next time he would try to keep it on paper!

Focus

1. What kind of painter was Alvin?
2. What were the colors in Alvin's masterpiece?
3. What did Alvin's masterpiece turn out to be?

THE MASTERPIECE BY ALVIN ARTWORK

Barbara saw a message in a painting of a tree. What did the message say? Let Barbara share her kind of art with you.

THEN I'LL BE AN ARTIST, TOO

Mary Emerson

When Barbara Morgan was a little girl, she had a favorite painting in her room. It was a picture of a tree. Every morning she lay in bed and stared at the painting. In the darkness of the early morning light, she saw many things. She saw that the tree trunk had thick dabs of paint that looked like bark. She saw that the small branches were done with light brush strokes. The painting seemed to be alive.

"Who painted my tree?" she asked her mother one day.

"Our Great Uncle Ben," her mother said. "He was an artist."

"Then I'll be an artist, too," Barbara said. She was only four years old!

As Barbara grew older, her interest in painting

also grew. Her parents helped her. They gave her paints and a special place to work. Years later she was still painting. Barbara worked hard at her painting. She studied art in college. After college she kept on painting.

Soon after Barbara left college she married Will Morgan. He was an artist too . . . a photographer. Together Barbara and Will toured the American Southwest. Barbara loved the Native American dances she saw there. The joy of the dance made

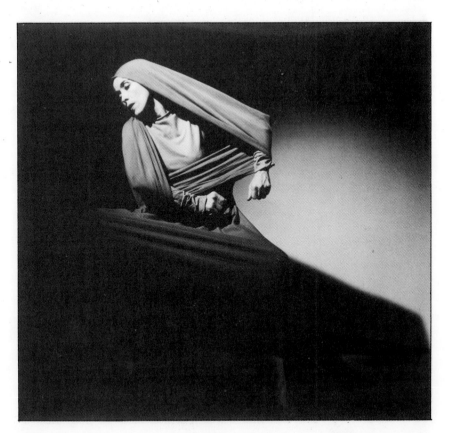

her happy. Later she was to meet another artist . . . a dancer who loved those same dances.

The Morgans then moved to New York City. Barbara began taking pictures in a museum of the art work done by friends. She found she could do exciting things with a camera, too. She became more and more interested in photography. It was a new kind of art when Barbara started. She had a lot of ideas about new ways of using her camera to put life into pictures.

In New York she met a dancer named Martha Graham. Martha was using some of the same dances Barbara had seen and loved in the Southwest! The two women became very good friends. Barbara took a few pictures of Martha's dancers. The camera was able to catch the motion of the dancers in midair. The pictures were beautiful and lifelike.

"Why not make a book of dance pictures?" Martha asked. Barbara liked the idea. For six years the two women worked together on making the book. The new pictures were even more beautiful. The women's book was a great success.

So Barbara made another book of pictures. It was about city children at summer camp. Her pictures of the campers were full of action, just like those of the dancers. Barbara tried to get action and joy into all of her pictures.

Barbara's photographs are of the world and the people in it. Her pictures capture the joy and action of life. She never forgot what her father told her years ago. "Remember," he said, "the world only seems to be motionless. . . . Everything is dancing and whirling about."

Focus

1. What made Barbara decide to be an artist? How old was she when she decided?
2. What was Barbara's work in New York? Why did she like it?
3. What were the subjects of Barbara's two books?

Many artists, like Barbara Morgan, use math when they work. They add, subtract, and measure.

Your math book helps you learn math. Here are some tips to help you with your math reading.

TAKE A FIRST LOOK

Take a first look at the math page printed here. What is the title at the top of the page? What does it tell you the page is about?

FIND THE KEY IDEAS

Notice that the page has three parts. The headings in dark type tell you what each part is about.

How many problems are in the first part? How many problems are in the second part?

How are the math problems in the third part different from the others? How many of these are you asked to solve?

Look at the picture on the page. Which problem does the picture go with?

READ CAREFULLY

Now you know that the page is about measurement. You know that you will add and subtract numbers. You also know that you will solve word problems.

MEASURE UP

Solve These Problems

1. How many centimeters equal 1 meter?

2. You want to take a picture of a spider. To get a clear picture, you must be at least 100 cm from your subject. How many meters must you stand from the spider?

Add These Numbers

3. 8 + 2 =   4. 3 + 9 =

5. 38 + 10 =   6. 83 + 6 =

Subtract These Numbers

7. 10 − 3 =   8. 8 − 2 =

9. 9 − 6 =   10. 11 − 1 =

237

Can you play the bells? Is your wigwag simply great? Well, Cotton Corners needs you in the Little Band.

The Little Band

Margaret Moore and John Travers Moore

Cotton Corners was a little town in the Southwest. The people were loyal to their hometown. They wanted to be proud of it. But

there was no one thing to be proud of . . . no famous park, no famous people, and certainly no fancy tall buildings. They really had nothing to be proud of . . . until the Little Band came along.

Right from the beginning Mr. Breen, the music teacher, knew it was a good little band. "You're a fine little band. You're even good enough to play for the new President."

"Why don't we?" asked Tommy, who played the tuba.

"We should," said Susie, who played the trumpet.

"It's our patriotic duty if we're that good," said Rosa, who beat the bass drum.

"Cotton Corners would be proud of us," cried Georgie. He carried the bells.

Pat, the piccolo player, said, "Let's go!"

Mario was the drum major. He tossed his baton high in the air. "I'll never drop my baton once," he promised.

"Not so fast," said the music teacher. "It takes money to go to Washington, D.C."

"But we could go on the trip somehow," said Mario.

"You have no uniforms," said Mr. Breen. "Besides, we haven't been invited to play."

"We can write a letter and ask," said Tommy.

"We can practice before and after school. We can be the best!" Rosa said.

"I think I know how we can get uniforms," offered Susie.

It was plain that the Little Band wanted to play in the President's Parade. Tommy wrote a wonderful letter to Washington.

When the answer to the letter came, it was a real surprise. The Little Band was welcome to march in the Inaugural Parade. The letter was from the Head of Parades.

"We're going!" Susie shouted. Georgie and Rosa and Pat and Tommy danced around, and Mario laughed and leaped.

The news spread quickly. Not a moment was wasted. The Mayor called a town meeting.

The Mayor spoke. "As sure as my name is Joan

Parker, we should support our Little Band. It's a great chance for us to show what a fine town Cotton Corners is."

The Little Band was excited. Would the people think that going to Washington was a good idea?

There was a buzz and a stir. The vote was taken. Then the final vote came. . . . "The Little Band is going to Washington. Everyone has agreed."

Now the Little Band had to raise money to pay for the trip.

The next two weeks sped by in Cotton Corners. The whole town tried to help the Little Band. The members of the band put up posters. They left cans in the bank for donations. They put an ad in the local newspaper.

Susie asked her parents to cut and sew the uniforms. She and her father made long slim blue pants. The coats her mother made were red satin with large gold buttons.

A concert was held the next Saturday evening to raise money. Every seat was taken. Seeing all those people made the Little Band think about what the trip to Washington meant. It wasn't just for the band alone . . . it was for Cotton Corners, too. The Little Band had to do its best.

The lights dimmed. Mr. Breen raised his baton. They played well. The crowd clapped and cheered. But the Little Band had only one thought in mind: had they earned enough money?

Yes, they had! There was more than enough.

Mr. Breen could go, and so could Susie's parents.

All the people in the town were pleased when they heard the good news. At last all was ready. Uniforms were pressed. Instruments were cleaned and polished.

The whole town came to the train station to see the Little Band off. Everybody waved as the whistle blew and the train pulled out. "See you on TV!" someone shouted.

The Little Band arrived in Washington. Everything was bustle and hustle. Susie, Mario, Georgie, Rosa, Tommy, Pat, Mr. Breen, and Susie's parents all went into the office of Mr. Gómez, the Head of Parades.

"Good morning," Mr. Gómez said to them. "What can I do for you?"

"We're here for the Inaugural Parade," Susie said. "You invited us."

"Yes, well. . . . Where did you say you were from?"

"Cotton Corners," Tommy said proudly.

"Oh, yes," said Mr. Gómez, running his finger down a list in front of him. "Hmmm. I don't find you listed. Let me look into this," he promised. Everyone was asking what had happened and what should be done. For some reason the Little Band was not expected, even though it had been invited.

The mistake was found on the desk of a man who was away. Mr. Gómez read a letter to himself.

245

He frowned. Then he shouted, "Cotton Corners! Now I know what happened. I thought someone said Cotta Commers. She's the famous bandleader. I expected her to come. I must have sent the letter to Cotton Corners by mistake."

"Well, I'm happy to welcome you anyway," Mr. Gómez said. "We need a band like yours for a good spot." He gave them careful directions. They were to bring up the rear!

The parade was led by a band from the President's home state. The people in the band were stepping in perfect time. Bands from state after state went by. There was color and

excitement. The bands all played very well. Each band seemed bigger and bigger until the Little Band came along.

All of a sudden something happened. The President whispered to a man beside him. That man gave orders to another man. That man gave orders to a motorcycle police officer. The police officer roared off to meet the Little Band.

"The President would like you to play for him," said the police officer. The Little Band marched right in front of the President. It was to be a command performance! Mario gave a nod. The Little Band broke into "Hail to the Chief," as any big band would do for the President.

When they finished, the President smiled and waved his hat. Newspaper reporters and a TV camera crew crowded about.

"Where are you from?" someone called. Mario answered in a voice that could be heard from coast to coast, "Cotton Corners!"

Now the people of Cotton Corners had something to be proud of . . . their own Little Band. Back home, the mayor was already planning a banner to be stretched across Main Street. The huge banner would say in large letters:

WELCOME TO COTTON CORNERS
HOME OF THE LITTLE BAND
THAT PLAYED A COMMAND PERFORMANCE
FOR THE PRESIDENT OF THE UNITED STATES

Focus

1. How did the Little Band decide to make the people of Cotton Corners proud?
2. How did they raise the money to get to Washington?
3. Was the Little Band expected at the Inaugural Parade? Why?
4. Did the President like the Little Band? How do you know?

Here's a chance to make music . . . with glasses filled with water. Better not get thirsty. You might swallow the tune.

MUSICAL GLASSES Kurt Dewey

Have you ever heard someone play a piano? A flute? A guitar? Many people play musical instruments. They have fun playing them and listening to them. What if you don't have a musical instrument? Don't worry, you can make your own easily.

You can make music with many things around the house. Anything large and empty can be a drum. Clay flowerpots can be hung upside down and tapped like bells. You can blow air into an empty bottle. A wood saw can be played with a bow!

An easy instrument to make is a set of musical glasses. You will need these things:

eight old drinking glasses

a pitcher of water

a felt marker

249

Choose the glasses you want by tapping them with a spoon or a pencil. A good musical glass should give a nice "ping" when you tap it. A glass that is too thick will make a sound like a dull thud. Put this thick glass away and look for a thinner one.

When you have eight glasses, line them up in a row. Now start with an empty one that has a low tone when you tap it. Place this glass at the beginning of the row. The tone of this glass will be the bottom or DO of your musical scale. Now with the pitcher pour water slowly into the second glass, tapping all the time. Listen to the tone. When your ear tells you that the tone is RE, stop pouring. Now go on to the third glass. Pour water from the pitcher into the glass until you hear the tone MI.

250

Pour water into the rest of the glasses. Be sure you tune each glass in turn as you go along. Your glasses should look like the ones on this page.

Can you make eight different tones from your glasses? If not, you may need to use some smaller glasses at the end of the scale. Are you happy with the eight tones of your musical scale? If you are, mark the water level on the outside of each glass with the felt marker. This will tell you how much water to pour into the different glasses the next time. Now number the glasses from 1 to 8.

Try to play a tune on your glasses. There are many different songs that you might try. Ask your friends to sing along as you play one of these songs. The number of the glass you tap is printed above each word.

Twinkle, Twinkle, Little Star

1 1   5 5   66   5
Twinkle, twinkle, little star,

4 4   3   3   2   2   1
How I wonder what you are.

5 5 4   4   3   3   2
Up above the world so high,

5   5 4   4   3   3   2
Like a diamond in the sky.

1   1   5 5   66   5
twinkle, twinkle, little star,

4   4   3   3   2   2   1
How I wonder what you are.

On Top of Old Smoky

1   1   3   5   8 6
On top of Old Smoky

6   4 5   6   5
All covered with snow,

1 1   3   5   5 2
I lost my true sweetheart

3   4   3   2 1
From courting too slow.

Focus

1. How many glasses are needed to make a simple instrument? Why are that many needed?

2. How do you make different notes with the glasses?

3. How do you play the glasses to make music?

253

CHECKPOINT

Vocabulary:
Word
Identification On your paper complete each sentence using words from the list on the right. One word will be left over.

1. Barbara Morgan used a _____.   college
2. Mario and Susie wore _____.   masterpiece
3. The Little Band played _____.   camera
4. The Little Band went to _____.   mayor
5. Alvin painted a _____.   uniforms
6. The Little Band sounded _____.   instruments
7. After high school some people   Washington
   go to _____.   fantastic
8. Barbara Morgan and Martha Graham   women
   are famous _____.

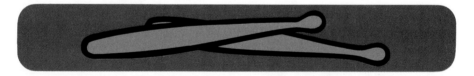

Vocabulary:
Vocabulary
Development
(synonyms and
antonyms) Letter your paper from *a* to *h*. Next to each letter write *S* if the words mean about the same thing. Write *O* if the words are opposites.

9. a. toward, away   e. little, small
   b. poster, picture   f. march, walk
   c. tall, short   g. in, out
   d. tired, sleepy   h. late, early

Read the paragraph below. Then answer the question.

Comprehension:
Author's
Purpose

There are many kinds of wind instruments. A tuba is a wind instrument that makes a big, deep sound. A flute makes a high, sweet sound. The sound of a trumpet is loud and bright.

10. What does this paragraph do?

    a. gives some facts   b. tells a funny tale

On your paper write each sentence below. Complete each sentence with one of the three words below it.

Decoding:
Suffixes -er,
-ment, -ness

11. After playing for the President, the Little Band got a _____.

    wilderness   compliment   fielder

12. Susie was a _____ in the Little Band.

    argument   trumpeter   sadness

13. Barbara Morgan was a _____.

    photographer   harness   moment

14. Washington is the capital of the United States _____.

    government   fondness   potter

15. A smile brings _____.

    happiness   layer   punishment

Everything's quiet. Not one sound can be heard. And you're sending a message! How do you do it?

SENDING MESSAGES

John Warren Stewig

Talk is everywhere. Listen! It's all around you. There are other ways to communicate our ideas, however. Our faces "tell" people how we feel. People don't always need to listen to what we say. Sometimes, they can just look at us. The way we look, stand, or move can send people a message about us that is unspoken.

Here is one way we send messages to "tell" people our ideas and feelings.

May I have some?   I'm sorry.   I know the answer.

Dancers tell us how they feel through motion. The motion of their bodies can tell us a whole story.

Pulling.

Round and round.

Strength.

Farm workers need to communicate across large fields. They use hand signals to communicate with each other.

Turn the lights on.   Turn the lights off.

When TV stars are doing a show, they watch the director. The director tells them what to do by using hand and arm motions.

Three minutes left.   Stretch it out—slow down.

Some deaf people learn a hand system of sending messages. Using this system, they can share ideas with other people.

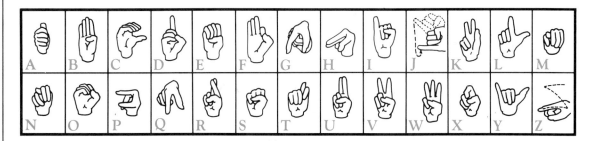

Another way people use a system to send messages is by using Morse code. It is made up of long sounds and short sounds. They are put together in patterns. Each pattern of long and short sounds stands for a letter of the alphabet.

You can send a message to someone else . . . to tell another person what you think or what you

feel. You can talk a message or write a message. But there are many other ways, like the ones shown here, to share your ideas. Can you think of any other ways to send messages?

Focus

1. Is talking the only way to send messages? What are three other ways?
2. How do some deaf people share their ideas?
3. How do you use sound to spell words in Morse code?
4. Tell one reason why it may be important to be able to send messages without words.

You know that there are many ways to send messages. Police use hand signals to direct traffic. Traffic signs also tell drivers what to do. If you ride a bicycle, you are a driver, so you should know what these signs mean. They are there to help you keep from being hurt.

Most traffic signs are easy to understand. What do you think this sign means? ✚ It warns you that there will be a crossroad soon. You should slow down and look both ways. Some signs use words instead of pictures. Here is an example: ◆STOP AHEAD◆ . It means that you are coming to a stop sign. You should slow down and get ready to stop.

Bicycle riders should also know how to use directional signals. These are hand signals like those that police use. Drivers use these signals to tell other drivers what they are going to do next.

This signal means that you are going to make a right turn.

This signal means that you are going to make a left turn.

This signal means that you are going to stop.

Now see if you can answer the questions below. Write your answers on a sheet of paper.

1. Why should a bicycle rider know what traffic signs mean?
2. What should you do if you see this sign ⬥STOP AHEAD⬥ ?
3. Draw the sign that means a crossroad is near. What should you do if you see this sign?
4. Draw the signal you would make if you were going to turn right. Draw the one for turning left.
5. Draw the signal you would use if you were about to stop.

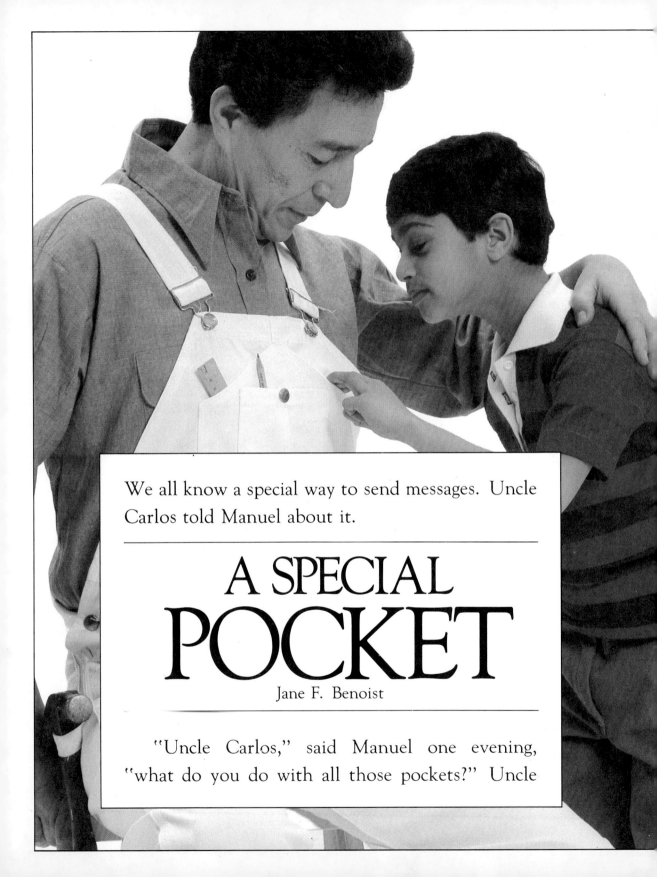

We all know a special way to send messages. Uncle Carlos told Manuel about it.

A SPECIAL
POCKET

Jane F. Benoist

"Uncle Carlos," said Manuel one evening, "what do you do with all those pockets?" Uncle

Carlos was sitting with Manuel on the steps outside his house.

Uncle Carlos slid his large, rough hands into the side pockets of his overalls. He wore overalls every workday. "Why, I carry many things in them, *niño*," he said. "When I'm up on a ladder, building a house, I keep my hammer in this loop. I carry nails in this pocket and a level in this one."

"What goes in the long, skinny pocket in the middle?" Manuel asked.

Uncle Carlos patted the deep pocket next to his heart. "I keep some special things in this one," he said. "It is never empty."

"Some special things?"

"Yes," said Uncle Carlos with a grin. "Would you like to see?"

Manuel nodded excitedly, but Uncle Carlos held up his hand. "I will show you what I keep here. But you must promise me something. If I share them with you, you must then share them with everyone you meet. Can you do that?"

Manuel thought a moment. "May I share them with Rosita?" he asked.

Uncle Carlos laughed. "Yes, share them with your sister and your friends, too," he said. "The more you share these, the more you will find in your pocket to give away."

"I promise to share them," Manuel said.

Uncle Carlos leaned closer. "All right. Watch closely, *chico*." He reached into the narrow space. Then he pulled out his hand and covered his mouth with it. When he took away his hand, there was nothing there . . . except a big, wide grin.

Manuel looked puzzled. Then he began to smile, too. "I know! You carry your smiles in that pocket."

"That's right," said Uncle Carlos. "That way they are always handy when I see your *mamá* or see a rainbow or meet someone who is lonely."

Manuel reached into his pocket and then he covered his face with a grin. "I promise to give these away, Uncle Carlos," he said. "But I'm going to save the biggest smile just for you."

Focus

1. What tools did Uncle Carlos carry in his overalls?
2. What did Manuel promise to do with the thing that was in Uncle Carlos's special pocket?
3. What was in Uncle Carlos's special pocket?

Primer Lesson

Look out how you use proud words.
When you let proud words go, it is not easy to call them back.
They wear long boots, hard boots; they walk off proud; they can't
    hear you calling—
Look out how you use proud words.

Carl Sandburg

There's an old song that says, "I've got the 日 in the morning and the 月 at night!" Read about Chinese picture-words to find out what you have to be happy about.

Messages from the East   John Jacobsen

Messages can be sent in many ways. One way to send messages, of course, is to write them down on paper. The Chinese started doing this thousands of years ago. Since that time Chinese writing has looked like pictures. When you look at a Chinese picture-word you cannot always tell what the word will sound like. You may know what it means, though.

Look at the way the Chinese wrote the word *sun* thousands of years ago: ☉ . It looked like a picture of the sun. But you cannot look at that picture and sound out the word *sun*.

Over the years Chinese writing has changed. Today the Chinese picture-word for sun looks like this: 日 . There are thousands of picture-words in Chinese writing. Would you like to read

Chinese? You would have to learn at least two thousand picture-words. You would also have to learn to read in a new way. People read Chinese in columns. They start reading at the top right hand corner and then read down. It is almost like adding.

Your library might have a Chinese newspaper. The picture-words are beautiful to look at . . . even if you can't read them. Chinese handwriting is an art. Chinese people often use brushes when writing picture-words.

You can write Chinese, too. Here are some Chinese numbers. See if you can write them. Use a pencil at first. Then you might want to try a brush. Maybe you can make a code and send a secret message to a friend using these Chinese numbers.

One 一

Two 二

Three 三

Four 四

Five 五

Six 六

Seven 七

Eight 八

Nine 九 Hundred 百

Ten 十 Thousand 千

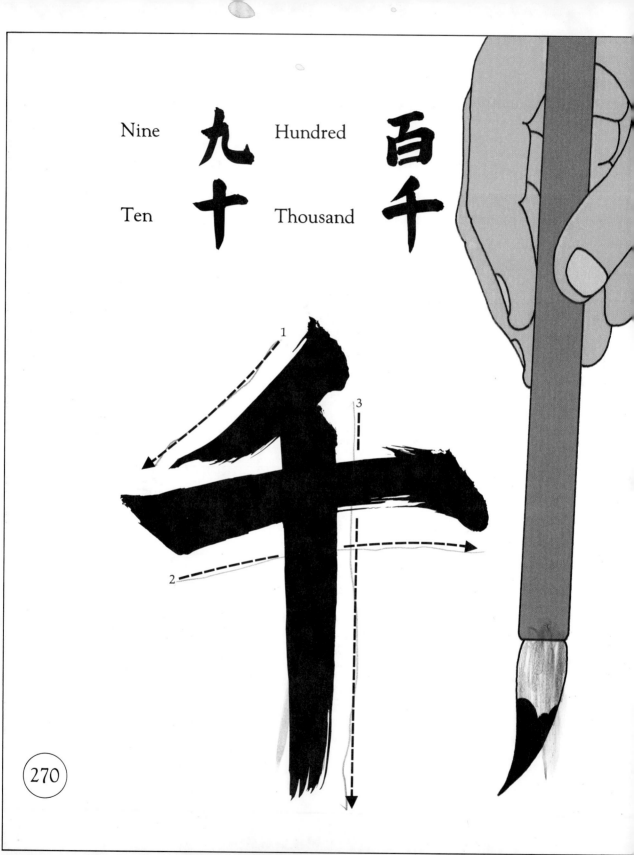

Now you can write all the figures. For instance, 1985:

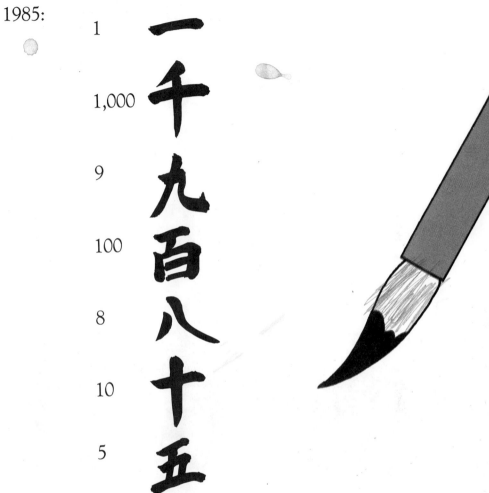

1
1,000
9
100
8
10
5

一千九百八十五

Focus

1. How many picture-words would you have to learn to read Chinese?
2. Why is Chinese writing like adding numbers?
3. Draw the Chinese picture-word for the number three.

271

Have you ever heard someone say, "It's all done with mirrors?" If not, keep it in mind when you read this story.

THE SECRET
THREE

Mildred Myrick

"Let's take a walk on the beach, Mark," said Billy. "The tide was high this morning. We may find something good on the sand." The two friends walked along the beach. They saw shells and a starfish. Billy spotted a green bottle in the seaweed on the beach.

"It's nothing but an old bottle," Mark said.

Billy picked up the bottle. "Look, Mark! There's a piece of paper inside the bottle and there's writing on it." Billy took the paper out of the bottle. "I think it's a message, but I can't read it."

Mark took the piece of paper, but he couldn't read the writing either.

The boys took the paper to Billy's house. They held the paper upside down. Then they held it right side up. They still couldn't read the writing.

"Maybe there's something on the other side," said Mark.

"No, there's nothing."

"Look in the mirror!" cried Billy. "Now we can read it!"

I live on the island. It would be fun to have a club with some friends who can read this writing.
Tom.

"Let's have a club!" Billy said.

"Yes! We can send secret messages to each other!" said Mark. "We could have a name for our club!" said Billy.

"Secret is a good word," said Mark. "And there are three of us."

"The Secret Three!" cried Billy.

"That's a great name!" Mark said. "I hope Tom likes it."

275

The boys showed the message to Billy's parents. "The new lighthouse keeper has a boy," said Billy's father. "Maybe this message is from him."

"Is the lighthouse on the island?" Mark asked.

"Yes, you can see it from here," said Billy. "Will Tom get a message if we send one in the bottle?"

"You can try it," said his mother. "This bottle came in with the high tide. Maybe the next tide will take it back."

"When is the next tide?" asked Mark.

"I know," said Billy. "The newspaper has a chart. Each day the tide is later. The tide was high on our beach at five o'clock this morning. It will be high again tonight about five thirty."

The boys worked on a secret message. They wrote the alphabet. They put one letter under the other. Then they gave each letter a number:

a	1	j	10	s	19
b	2	k	11	t	20
c	3	l	12	u	21
d	4	m	13	v	22
e	5	n	14	w	23
f	6	o	15	x	24
g	7	p	16	y	25
h	8	q	17	z	26
i	9	r	18		

They put the message in the bottle and took it to the beach. They were just in time—the tide was starting to go out. When they could no longer see the bottle, Billy and Mark went home.

They looked in the newspaper to find out the time of the next high tide. It was to be at six o'clock the next morning. Billy and Mark were at the beach at six o'clock on the dot. They walked a long time, but they did not find the bottle.

After supper the boys looked again. They met a fishing crew working on a boat. "Are you looking for something?" asked one of them.

"We're looking for a green bottle," said Billy.

"I hope you find it," said another.

Mark and Billy walked on. Then Mark ran toward something on the beach. It was the green bottle!

"Hurry, Billy!" cried Mark. "There's the bottle, and it has a paper inside it!"

"You're right!" Billy said. "It is our bottle, and there's a message inside! I can see the writing!" They opened the bottle and took out the paper.

Billy took a mirror from his pocket. The message said: I had fun with your message. The Secret Three sounds like a good name. We can meet on Tuesday. Please come with the fishing crew. Tom

"Let's go to the island and see Tom," said Billy. "We can ask the fishing crew now." They told the crew about the club. The crew agreed to take the boys to the island if they asked their parents.

"When we get to the island, how will we know which boy is Tom?" Mark asked.

"We could have a secret sign and a secret handshake. When someone gives the secret sign and the secret handshake, we will know he's Tom," said Billy. The boys sent Tom this message:

Dear Tom,
Here is our secret sign.
One club member holds
up 19-9-24 fingers. That
stands for the 19-9-24
letters in "secret." The next
member holds up 20-8-
18-5-5 fingers. That
stands for the three club
members. The secret
handshake is to shake
hands with the 12-5-6-20
hands.   2-9-12-12-25
                        and
                13-1-18-11

They put the message in the bottle, and the tide took it out. On Tuesday they met the fishing crew at the beach. When they got near the island, they saw a boy on shore.

"That may be Tom," said Billy, "but we've got to be sure. We'll give the secret sign."

Mark and Billy jumped out of the boat. The boy ran to meet them. Billy held up six fingers. The boy held up three fingers. The boys knew who it was!

"I'm Tom," the boy said, "and am I glad to see you!"

"I'm Billy, and this is Mark," said Billy. They shook hands with their left hands.

The Secret Three held its first meeting that day.

Focus

1. Where did Billy and Mark find the first message?
2. How did they read the message?
3. Whom was the message from? Where did the writer of the message live?
4. Why did the boys decide to call the club The Secret Three?
5. How did the boys recognize Tom?

CHECKPOINT

Read these sentences and the words under each. On your paper write each sentence with the word that fits in it.

1. Tom lived on an _____.

   island   image   unspoken   alphabet

2. The _____ will be high at noon.

   pocket   tide   puzzled   picture-words

3. _____ is fun to learn.

   Chinese   Manuel   Tuesday   Lighthouse

Read the paragraph below. On your paper answer the questions that follow.

Mark, Billy, and Tom formed a club called The Secret Three. Their club was like many others because many clubs have secret signs and handshakes. But their club was different from most clubs because it met on an island.

4. How are clubs alike?

   a. Most have three members.

   b. Most have a secret sign or handshake.

5. How was The Secret Three different from most clubs?

   a. The Secret Three met on an island.

   b. The Secret Three had a secret sign.

284

Look at the list of words below. Fill in each blank with a word from the list. Write the completed sentences on your paper.

experiment   safer   kindness   cement

6. Something that is more safe is _____.

7. You may want to _____ with writing Chinese.

8. Everybody likes to be treated with _____.

Look at the signs below. Answer the questions that follow.

9. Would you go down the road if you saw the first sign?

10. How fast may a car go past the second sign?

11. What will you soon cross after seeing the third sign?

12. If you see the last sign, which way will you soon be going?

THE MOON SINGER

Clyde Robert Bulla

Long ago, in a far country, there lived a miller and his wife. One day a woman came to the mill, leading a child by the hand.

"Take this boy," she said. "I can no longer care for him."

"Another mouth to feed? Oh, no," said the miller.

"Then," said the woman, "at least give us a place to rest tonight."

The miller gave them a bed of straw in the mill shed. In the morning the woman was gone. The child was left behind.

"This is not so bad," said the miller's wife. "He may be a help to us later on."

"That's true," said the miller. So they kept the boy and called him Torr, which was a short name and easy to remember.

He grew tall and strong, and he worked about the mill.

But he was a strange boy.

Sometimes he forgot his work and wandered off into the woods. There he would stand, listening, as if he heard something no one else could hear.

Sometimes at night he left his bed and stood for hours under the sky.

On a summer night the miller and his wife wakened to the sound of singing. The voice was clear and high. The song was one they had never heard before.

They went to the window.

"It's Torr!" said the miller's wife.

The boy was standing in the moonlight. He was singing, with his face turned toward the sky.

The miller ran out in his nightshirt. "Stop your noise!" he said. "You'll wake the whole village!"

He brought Torr inside. He scolded him and told him never to do it again.

After that the boy sang no more where the miller and his wife might hear. Late at night he went deep into the woods, and there he sang.

A hunter heard him and drew near to listen. Afterward he talked in the village of the boy who sang. "His music sends chills down my spine," he said, "but I would go a long way to hear it."

Others went to the woods to listen.

"The boy is odd," said some of them. "He may

bring harm to us."

"He has a great gift," said the old music-master who lived in the village. "He cannot sing at home, so he sings in the woods, and where is the harm in that?"

One evening a stranger came to the village. A wheel of his carriage had broken. While it was being mended, he stopped at the inn.

Villagers gathered to see him. He was so richly dressed that they were sure he must be a fine gentleman.

One of them asked, "Sir, are you a lord?"

The man laughed. "As a matter of fact, I am," he said. "I am Lord Crail, from the court of the queen."

"Ah!" said the people, all together. A woman asked, "Is the queen as beautiful as they say?"

"Even more beautiful," said Lord Crail.

"And is the palace really so splendid?" asked the woman.

"The most splendid of all palaces," said Lord Crail.

"I once heard," said the woman, "of a baker who made such pies that he was taken to the palace to bake for the queen."

"This is true enough," said Lord Crail. "And the best storytellers in the land, the best music makers, actors, and dancers are all at the palace. If they do not come to us, we find them and bring them there."

The old music-master had come to the inn with the others. He asked, "My lord, does the queen have need of a singer?"

"There are singers at court," said Lord Crail, "but the queen has grown weary of them. She says their songs all sound the same." He asked, "Is there a singer in your village?"

"There is, my lord," said the music-master. "He is a boy who sings in the woods at night."

"That boy is odd!" said some of the others.

"I find nothing odd about him," said the music-master. "His voice touches the heart, and the songs he sings are like no other songs."

"When may I hear him?" asked Lord Crail.

"He sings in the woods when the moon is shining," said the music-master. "The moon will be shining tonight."

"Take me to hear him," said Lord Crail.

They went together to the woods.

"Just ahead is a bridge over the stream," said the

291

292

music-master. "The boy often goes there to sing."

"Listen!" said Lord Crail.

Deep in the woods the boy was singing. There were no words to the song. The tune rose and fell and rose again, like the song of a bird.

Lord Crail started forward. Dry sticks cracked under his feet. When he reached the bridge, the boy was gone.

"He heard us and ran away," said the music-master. "He is very shy."

"I must find him," said Lord Crail.

"Nothing easier," said the music-master. "He works at the mill."

The next day Lord Crail went to the mill. There he found Torr carrying sacks of flour into the shed.

"I heard you sing last night," said Lord Crail.

Torr looked away.

"Come, don't be afraid," said Lord Crail. "Who taught you to sing?"

"No one," answered Torr.

"Where do you learn your songs?" asked Lord Crail.

"They come to me," said the boy. "When I'm alone they come to me."

"Why do you hide away in the woods?" asked

Lord Crail. "Why not sing where everyone can hear you?"

Torr looked surprised. "Who would want to hear me?" he asked.

"Perhaps the queen herself," said Lord Crail. "Today I shall take you away from here. We shall go to Her Majesty."

"Where?" asked Torr.

"To the palace," said Lord Crail. "To the queen."

The miller had been listening. He spoke up. "My lord, how can we ever thank you? My wife and I have brought up the boy as if he were our own. We always knew there were great things in store for him. Tell me, will he live in the palace?"

"Most likely," said Lord Crail.

"Will he be paid well?" asked the miller.

"He will live like a prince," said Lord Crail.

"Do you hear?" said the miller to the boy. "And when you are living like a prince, think of my wife and me, who were always so kind to you."

The carriage came for Torr and Lord Crail. Torr had no time to think. He could not believe what was happening. On the long journey his head was in a whirl.

They came to the palace with its stone walls and great iron gates.

Lord Crail led the way down a long hall and into a room. "You will sleep here," he said.

But Torr could not sleep. The bed was too large and too soft. The air was heavy. It was hard for him to breathe.

In the morning servants came into the room. They combed his hair and curled it with hot irons. They fitted him into a tight suit of crimson velvet. They pushed his feet into shoes that pinched his toes.

Lord Crail came in.

"Now," he said, "you are ready to meet the queen."

Torr followed him up the stairs and into the music room. Lords and ladies were there. The queen sat among them, in a chair higher than those of the others. She was young and lovely. Her dark hair was caught up in a gold band that looked like a crown.

Torr knelt before her, as he had been told to do.

"Lord Crail says he found you singing to the moon," she said. "Will you sing to me now?"

Torr stood before the queen. He felt cold, and

295

he trembled. He opened his mouth, and no sound came.

"Sing!" said Lord Crail in a fierce whisper.

Again Torr tried. His throat was dry, and no song came to him.

Lord Crail bowed to the queen. "Your Majesty, the boy is not quite ready," he said. "After he has rested, I promise you he will sing even better than ever. Let me bring him before you tomorrow."

He took Torr away.

The next day they went back to the music room. The queen was there alone.

"I thought it might be easier," she said, "if the boy sang only for me."

"Your Majesty is most kind," said Lord Crail. He said to Torr, "Sing."

"I can't!" said Torr.

"You must!" said Lord Crail.

Torr's mouth opened. One strange sound came out, like the croaking of a frog.

Lord Crail took Torr's arm and led him away. He said to the boy, when they were alone, "I brought you here. I promised the queen you would sing such songs as she had never heard before. Why have you made a fool of me?"

Torr said nothing.

"Answer me!" said Lord Crail.

"I—don't know," said Torr.

"You don't know—you don't know!" said Lord Crail. "Is that all you can say? The queen was waiting. I was waiting. You have made a fool of me!" He went away.

Soon a servant came into the room. He stripped off Torr's velvet suit and gave him back the clothes he had worn to the palace.

"What am I to do?" asked Torr.

"You're to go," said the servant.

Torr left the palace. He went out into the city. All about him were horses and carriages and crowds of people.

He walked up one street and down another. He tried to find his way out of the city. At last he was in the country, on the road that led to his village.

At night he slept by the road. Toward the end of the next day he was back in his village.

He went to the mill. The miller and his wife were there. They were painting a sign to hang over the door.

Once the mill had had no name. Now they had given it one. They were painting the sign to read:

"The Mill of the Queen's Singer."

They stared at Torr.

"You're home!" said the miller's wife.

"Why aren't you in the palace?" asked the miller.

"They sent me away," said Torr.

"Didn't you go there to be the queen's singer?" asked the miller.

"Yes," said Torr, "but—I couldn't sing."

"Why not?" asked the miller's wife.

"I don't know," said Torr. "The walls shut me in, and the air pressed down on me, and I couldn't sing."

"You didn't try," said the miller. "You had no trouble singing before. Then when you had this great chance, you didn't try."

"You must go back," said the miller's wife.

"No," said Torr. "I can't ever go back."

"What shall we do?" cried the miller's wife. "We've told everyone our boy is singer to the queen. We even named the mill for him. After all our years of hard work, we thought life was going to be easier." She said to Torr, "All you've done for us is make us look like fools. Now you can go!"

"Yes, go!" said the miller.

299

"Where?" asked Torr.

"I don't care," said the miller. "Just go!"

Angrily he waved his paintbrush. The paint from the brush splashed Torr from head to foot.

He turned and ran.

He ran out of the village. He was a strange, wild-looking figure with green paint on his face and clothes.

"See the green-faced scarecrow!" people said, and they drove him away.

He hid in barns and haystacks. He ate what little food he could find—a few berries here, a sour apple there.

He came to the hill country where shepherds cared for their flocks. He was ill and half starved. He lay down to rest.

A storm came. Still he lay there, too ill to move.

A shepherd and his wife found him and carried him to their hut. The shepherd's wife fed him. The shepherd scrubbed the last of the paint from his face.

Torr stayed in the hut until he grew strong again. He helped the shepherds care for their sheep.

Sometimes he remembered the mill and the miller and his wife. He remembered Lord Crail and the palace and the queen. Always he tried to put these thoughts out of his mind. They were like bad dreams to him now.

The shepherds were kind to him. He liked to be among the sheep and lambs, and he made friends with the shepherds' dogs.

He said to himself, "I am happy here."

Yet it was not true. He was not quite happy. Over and over he asked himself the reason.

One night he could not sleep. He went out into the woods. The moon was bright. A breeze blew, and he could smell the leaves and grass and the sea beyond.

Suddenly he was happy. He thought he had never been so happy before. A song had come to him.

He began to sing. His voice was clear. It was stronger and deeper than before. He wanted to go leaping from hill to hill. He wanted to shout, "I can sing—I can sing again!"

For half the night he sang. The shepherds came to their doors and listened in wonder.

Night after night Torr sang.

Word traveled across the land of the singing shepherd boy. A traveler brought the word to Lord

Crail at the queen's palace.

"He sings at night?" asked Lord Crail.

"Yes," said the traveler. "They call him the moon singer, because they say he sings to the moon."

"Does he have another name?" asked Lord Crail.

"Yes," said the traveler. "It is Torr."

Lord Crail went to the queen. "Do you remember the boy who came here to sing, Your Majesty?" he asked. "The one who opened his mouth and croaked like a frog?"

"I remember him well," said the queen.

"He was only pretending," said Lord Crail. "All the time he could sing. He is singing now in another part of the country."

"Why should he pretend he could not sing?" asked the queen.

"I mean to find out," said Lord Crail. "I mean to bring him here again. If he dares to pretend, he will be punished in a way he won't forget."

"The boy did not seem to be pretending," said the queen.

"Your Majesty, he must have been," said Lord
Crail.

"I can't believe it," said the queen, "and as much as I wish to hear him, it doesn't seem right to bring him here again."

"Then how can you hope to hear him?" asked Lord Crail.

"I could go to him, instead," she said.

"Your Majesty!" cried Lord Crail. "You could not do that!"

"Surely the queen may do as she wishes," she said. "I have stayed so long inside these walls that I am weary of them. Find out where the boy lives, and we shall go there."

So it was that the queen set out on a journey with two ladies of the court, Lord Crail, and three servants.

They traveled until they came to the hill country. Then they hid the royal coach in an old barn. They dressed in the plain clothes of country people.

They found the house where Torr lived. The queen said to the shepherd, "We have heard of the boy who sings. When may we hear him?"

"In a little while, when the moon rises," said the shepherd. "Take the path to the clearing in the woods. Many go there to listen, but they keep themselves hidden, because the boy is shy."

The queen and her party went down the path and into the woods. When they came to the clearing, they waited in the shadows. Others were waiting, too. Shepherds were there with their wives and children.

The moon rose. By its light they saw the boy in the clearing. He began to sing.

"Oh—beautiful!" whispered the queen.

"You see," Lord Crail whispered back. "All the time he could sing. He shall be brought to the palace and—"

"No," said the queen. "Can't you see? He belongs here."

"But Your Majesty, you have a right to hear him whenever you wish," said Lord Crail.

"So I do," said the queen, "and so I shall. Hush! He's beginning again."

Torr's song floated up through the woods. It was a song of the night—of the moon and the stars and mist over the sea.

"Beautiful!" the queen whispered again.

So she listened, that night and many another night. And Torr sang his songs, never knowing she was near.

GLOSSARY

Full pronunciation key*   The pronunciation of each word is shown just after the word, in this way: ab·bre·vi·ate (ə brē′vē āt).

The letters and signs used are pronounced as in the words below.

The mark ′ is placed after a syllable with primary or heavy accent, as in the example above.

The mark ′ after a syllable shows a secondary or lighter accent, as in **ab·bre·vi·a·tion** (ə brē′vē ā′shən).

a	hat, cap	**k**	kind, seek	**TH**	then, smooth
ā	age, face	**l**	land, coal	**u**	cup, butter
ä	father, far	**m**	me, am	**u̇**	full, put
b	bad, rob	**n**	no, in	**ü**	rule, move
ch	child, much	**ng**	long, bring	**v**	very, save
d	did, red	**o**	hot, rock	**w**	will, woman
e	let, best	**ō**	open, go	**y**	young, yet
ē	equal, be	**ô**	order, all	**z**	zero, breeze
ėr	term, learn	**oi**	oil, voice	**zh**	measure, seizure
f	fat, if	**ou**	house, out	**ə**	represents:
g	go, bag	**p**	paper, cup		a in about
h	he, how	**r**	run, try		e in taken
i	it, pin	**s**	say, yes		i in pencil
ī	ice, five	**sh**	she, rush		o in lemon
j	jam, enjoy	**t**	tell, it		u in circus
		th	thin, both		

*Pronunciation Key and respellings are from *Scott, Foresman Intermediate Dictionary* by E. L. Thorndike and Clarence L. Barnhart. Copyright © 1979 by Scott, Foresman and Company. Reprinted by permission.

A

ac·tion (ak'shən) *noun.* 1. something that is done. 2. the act of doing something.

Ae·sop (ē'səp or ē'sop) *noun.* a Greek author who wrote fables.

Al·man·zo (äl mon'zō) *noun.* a male name.

A·mel·ia (ə mē'lya) *noun.* a female name.

A·mer·i·ca (ə mer'ə kə) *noun.* 1. the United States of America. 2. North America. 3. South America.

an·swer (an'sər) *noun.* solution to a problem: The correct *answer* to the math problem is five. —*verb.* to reply in words or by writing.

Ar·i·on (ar'ē ən) *noun.* a male name.

art (art) *noun.* painting, drawing, or sculpture: My aunt teaches *art* at the museum.

art·ist (ar'tist) *noun.* one who paints, draws, or sculpts.

B

Bar·bar·a (bar'bə rə) *noun.* a female name.

Bir·die (bėrd'ē) *noun.* a last name.

Blan·chard (blan'chėrd) *noun.* a last name.

bor·row (bor'ō) *verb.* 1. to take something from another person knowing you must give it back: The softball team always *borrows* two bats. 2. to adopt as one's own; take.

both·er (boŦH'ər) *verb.* to annoy; to trouble: Don't *bother* me when I'm reading a book.

brake (brāk) *noun.* a device used to slow down a moving vehicle: Barbara put on the *brake* to stop her bicycle.

build·ing (bil'ding) *verb.* making things: The bird was *building* a nest. —*noun.* thing that is built, for example, a store or house.

C

cam·er·a (kam'ər ə) *noun.* a device that takes movies or photographs.

can·non (kan'ən) *noun.* a big gun supported by wheels: A *cannon* makes a loud noise. **—cannons** or **cannon** *plural.*

card·board (kärd'bôrd') *noun.* a stiff paper used to make boxes. *—adjective.* made of cardboard.

Car·los (kär'lōs) *noun.* a male name.

Char·lie (Chär'lē) *noun.* a nickname for Charles; a male name.

Chi·ca·go (shə kô'gō or shə kä'gō) *noun.* a large city in Illinois.

chim·ney (chim'nē) *noun.* a pipe through which smoke from a fire rises.

Chi·nese (chī nēz') *adjective.* having to do with the country of China, its language, or the people.

Chris·to·pher (Kris'tə fər) *noun.* a male name.

chuck·le (chuk'əl) *verb.* to laugh quietly: It was easy to *chuckle* at the comedian's jokes.

club·house (klub'hous') *noun.* a building used for meetings by a special group of people: The baseball team met in the *clubhouse.*

col·lege (kol'ij) *noun.* a school that comes after high school: During *college* Carlos studied mathematics.

con·test (kon'test) *noun.* competition; game where a person or group of people try to win: Many people entered the chess *contest.*

court·yard (kôrt'yärd) *noun.* an enclosed area in or near a building: The small *courtyard* contains many flowering shrubs.

cous·in (kuz'n) *noun.* son or daughter of one's aunt or uncle. **cousins.**

creek (krēk or krik) *noun.* a small stream.

crumb (krum) *noun.* a little bit of something: Just a *crumb* of cake was left.

D

danc·er (dan'sər) *noun.* one who dances: A ballet *dancer* spends hours practicing.

dia·mond (dī'mənd or dī'ə mənd) *noun.* 1. a precious, valuable hard stone: The gleaming *diamond* made a lovely ring. 2. a figure having four equal sides and angles. 3. a baseball field.

di·ar·y (dī'ər ē) *noun.* 1. a written record of what one has done each day. 2. a book in which to write this record. **diaries.**

dif·fer·ent (dif'ər ənt) *adjective.* unlike; not like another: I am very *different* from my brother.

dol·phin (dol'fən) *noun.* a sea animal related to the whale.

dough (dō) *noun.* a soft, thick mixture of flour and liquid from which bread and pastry are made: The bread *dough* is rising very quickly.

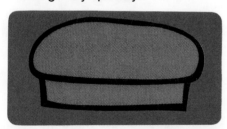

E

ear·ly (ėr'lē) *adjective.* 1. in the first part: *Early* morning is the coolest part of the day. 2. before the regular time. **earlier, earliest.**

earth (ėrth) *noun.* 1. (Earth) planet where we live. 2. dirt; ground. 3. dry land.

el·e·phant (el'ə fənt) *noun.* largest land animal alive, with a trunk and long ivory tusks.

F

fa·mous (fā'məs) *adjective.* well known; important: The *famous* dancer was cheered by the large audience.

fan·tas·tic (fan tas'tik) *adjective.* 1. highly imaginative; strange, wild. 2. (informal) marvelous; wonderful: I thought that the play was *fantastic*!

fic·tion (fik'shən) *noun.* something that is untrue or make-believe: The stories she told were all *fiction*.

fin·ish (fin'ish) *noun.* the end. —*verb.* to complete.

fog (fog) *noun.* thick mist; cloud of fine drops of water.

fold (fōld) *noun.* a line made by creasing: He made a *fold* in the fabric.

fol·low (fol'ō) *verb.* 1. to come after: The large dog *follows* the cat everywhere. 2. obey.

fo·rest (fôr'ist) *noun.* an area in which trees and plants grow close together.

for·tune (fôr'chən) *noun.* a lot of money; riches: The jewels were worth a *fortune.*

foun·tain pen (foun'tən pen) *noun.* pen that has a steady supply of ink running through a tube inside the pen.

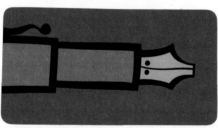

G

Gar·rett (gar'it) *noun.* a male name.

gen·er·ous (jen'ər əs) *adjective.* unselfish; kind: The *generous* boy shared his sandwich with a friend.

Greek (grēk) *noun.* a person from Greece. **Greeks.**

grin (grin) *noun.* a broad smile: A large *grin* appeared on Billy's face as he left school for summer vacation.

H

half (haf) *noun.* 1. one of two equal parts: *Half* of the cake was eaten. 2. a part of. **halves.**

hand·shake (hand'shāk') *noun.* an act of grasping one's hand in friendship or greeting.

haunt·ed (hôn'tid) *adjective.* visited by ghosts; spooky: The children peeked in the windows of the *haunted* house.

hay·loft (hā'lôft') *noun.* a place in a barn where hay is kept.

heart (härt) *noun.* 1. part of the body that pumps blood. 2. kindness. 3. the middle.

home·work (hōm'wėrk') *noun.* lessons to be done at home.

horse (hôrs) *noun.* four-legged animal with a mane and a tail.

hu·man (hyü'mən) *noun.* a person. —*adjective.* having to do with people: Arms and legs are parts of the *human* body.

I

i·mag·ine (i maj'ən) *verb.* to form a picture in one's mind: Try to *imagine* what you'll be doing in ten years. **imagined, imagining.**

in·stru·ment (in'strə mənt) *noun.* 1. a thing that makes musical sounds: The drum and piano are Peter's favorite musical *instruments.* 2. tool.

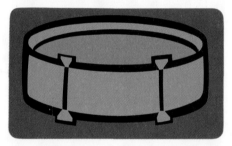

in·vis·i·ble (in viz'ə bəl) *adjective.* not able to be seen: Air is *invisible.*

is·land (ī'lənd) *noun.* piece of land surrounded on all sides by water: We had to take a boat to the *island.*

J

jew·el (jü'əl) *noun.* precious stone; gem: The queen had many *jewels* in her crown.

Jo·sé (hō zā') *noun.* a male name.

K

knead (nēd) *verb.* to press, fold, and squeeze, especially bread dough. **kneaded, kneading.**

L

Lau·ra (Lôr'ə) *noun.* a female name.

lem·on·ade (lem'ə nād') *noun.* a drink made of lemon juice, sugar, and water.

light·house (līt'hous') *noun.* a tower with a bright light to warn ships of a dangerous area.

lute (lüt) *noun.* an old stringed instrument played by plucking the strings.

M

mag·ni·fy·ing (mag'nə fī'ing) *adjective.* making something look larger than it is: The children looked at tiny insects through a *magnifying* glass.

Maj·es·ty (maj'ə stē) *noun.* a title used for a king and queen: "Your *Majesty,* please accept this gift," said the servant.

man·ner (man'ər) *noun.* 1. way of doing something. 2. (plural) polite behavior. **manners.**

311

Man·uel (Man wel′) *noun.* a male name.

Mar·i·o (Mär′ē ō) *noun.* a male name.

Mar·sha (Mär′sha) *noun.* a female name.

mas·ter·piece (mas′tər pēs′) *noun.* 1. a person's best piece of work: The painting on display was the artist's *masterpiece.* 2. anything done very well.

may·or (mā′ər) *noun.* head of city government: City elections for the office of *mayor* are tomorrow.

min·ute (min′it) *noun.* sixty seconds: There are sixty *minutes* in an hour.

N

nar·row-necked (nar′ō nekt′) *adjective.* having a thin neck: The spoon was stuck in the *narrow-necked* bottle.

neigh·bor (nā′bər) *noun.* someone who lives next door or nearby: My next–door *neighbor* is very friendly.

note·book (nōt′bùk′) *noun.* a blank book in which to write things so that they can be remembered or learned.

O

of·ten (ô′ fən) *adverb.* frequently: In Mexico it *often* rains in the afternoon.

o·range (ôr′inj) *noun.* 1. a round, reddish-yellow citrus fruit of a tree grown in a warm climate, used for juice. 2. a reddish-yellow color: The color of the setting sun was *orange.*

ov·en (uv′ən) *noun.* a small space in a stove for baking and roasting.

own (ōn) *verb.* to have; to possess.

P

palm tree (päm trē) *noun.* type of tree, with a tall trunk and large leaves, that grows in a warm climate.

pa·rade (pə rād') *noun.* large procession or march.

Par·see (pär'sē) *noun.* a wise man.

pen·cil (pen'səl) *noun.* a thin, pointed tool used for writing or drawing.

per·son (pėr'sən) *noun.* a human being; man, woman, or child.

pic·ture-word (pik'chər wėrd') *noun.* a way of saying things and ideas through drawings.

pitch·er (pich'ər) *noun.* a container made of glass or china with a spout used for holding liquids: The *pitcher* was filled with milk.

plain (plān) *noun.* 1. a flat stretch of land: Cattle wandered over the *plains.* 2. easy to understand. 3. without decoration.

plan·et (plan'it) *noun.* a heavenly body that moves around a sun: It is hard to imagine what life would be like on another *planet.*

po·et (pō'it) *noun.* a person who writes poems.

po·lice (pə lēs') *noun.* persons whose job is to keep order in a town or city.

praise (prāz) *noun.* good things said about someone: Everyone gave *praise* to the winners.

pres·ent (prez' nt) *noun.* a gift.

pret·ty (prit'ē) *adjective.* attractive; beautiful. **prettier, prettiest.**

Q

queen (kwēn) *noun.* a female leader of a country or state.

R

rac·coon (ra kün') *noun.* small grayish-brown animal with markings around the eyes and a ringed tail.

ra·di·a·tor (rā'dē ā'tər) *noun.* 1. a device for heating a room: The *radiator* in the kitchen heated the first floor. 2. device used to cool water, such as the car radiator.

rare (rer or rar) *adjective.* 1. not often found; unusual. 2. very special; unusually good: It is *rare* to find an unfriendly dolphin. **rarer, rarest.**

rea·son (rē′zn) *noun.* 1. cause. 2. explanation: Charlie had two *reasons* for being late.

re·ceive (ri sēv′) *verb.* 1. to get: Jeff will *receive* a new bicycle for his birthday. 2. to let into your mind; accept. **received, receiving.**

re·ward (ri wôrd′) *noun.* a payment made for something done: He deserved a *reward* for his honesty.

rhi·no (rī′nō) *noun.* a nickname for a rhinoceros.

rhi·noc·er·os (rī nos′ər əs) *noun.* a large animal of Africa and Asia with one or two horns on the nose. **—rhinoceroses** or **rhinoceros** *plural.*

Rob·in (rob′ən) *noun.* a person's name.

Ro·man (rō′mən) *noun.* a person from Rome. **Romans.**

S

sail·or (sā′lər) *noun.* a person who works on a sailboat or other ship.

scale (skāl) *noun.* a series of tones in music: She was practicing a *scale* on her violin.

scis·sors (siz′ərz) *noun.* a tool for cutting made of two sharp blades fastened so that they can close together on material to be cut. **—scissors** *plural.*

search (sėrch) *verb.* to look for: Maria *searched* for her lost dog.

serve (sėrv) *verb.* 1. to put food and drink on table: Mother will *serve* soup for lunch. 2. to work for. **served, serving.**

sew·ing (sō′ing) *noun.* 1. work done with a needle and thread. 2. something needing to be sewed. **—adjective.** having to do with sewing: a *sewing* machine.

ship (ship) *noun.* a large boat that goes in deep water. — *verb.* to send from one place to another. **shipped, shipping.**

shop (shop) *noun.* 1. a small place where items are sold. 2. a place where things are made or repaired: The shoe repair *shop* opens at nine o'clock.

shoul·der (shōl'dər) *noun.* a part of the body to which the arm or wing is attached: The little girl sat on her father's *shoulder* to see the show.

skip·per (skip'ər) *noun.* 1. a kind of fish; a mud skipper. 2. captain of a boat.

sneak·er (snē'kər) *noun.* canvas shoe with rubber sole, used in sport activities. **sneakers.**

some·bod·y (sum'bod'ē) *noun.* someone; any person.

sort (sôrt) *noun.* kind; type: This *sort* of fruit is my favorite. —*verb.* to arrange in order.

South·west (south'west') *adjective.* between the south and the west. —*noun.* area that is in the southwest: Texas and Arizona are in the *Southwest.*

square (skwer or skwar) *noun.* 1. an open space in a city, usually planted with grass and trees: The fair was being held on the city *square.* 2. figure with four equal sides.

state (stāt) *noun.* group of people in an area organized under one government: Texas is a large *state.*

stir (stėr) *verb.* 1. to mix by moving with a spoon or fork: *Stir* the cake batter well. 2. to blend. 3. to move around.

stork (stôrk) *noun.* a large wading bird that has long legs, a long neck, and a long bill.

sto·ry·tell·er (stôr'ē tel'ər) *noun.* one who tells stories and tales.

Stue·y (stü'ē) *noun.* nickname for Stuart; a male name.

sud·den·ly (sud'n lē) *adverb.* all of a sudden; quickly: *Suddenly* the dog began to bark loudly.

sup·port (sə pôrt') *noun.* 1. help; aid. 2. person or thing that holds something up: The beams were *support* for the house.

315

sup·pose (sə pōz′) *verb.* 1. to think; imagine. 2. to consider as a possibility: I *suppose* I could go if I finish my homework. **supposed, supposing.**

Sus·ie (süz′ē) *noun.* a female name, usually short for Susan.

sys·tem (sis′təm) *noun.* 1. a plan or method: Ruth has a good *system* for getting her homework done. 2. an ordered group of beliefs.

T

ta·ble·spoon (tā′bəl spün′) *noun.* 1. unit of measure used in cooking equal to three teaspoons. 2. a large serving spoon. **tablespoons.**

tame (tām) *adjective.* 1. taken from a wild state and trained to live with humans. 2. gentle: The *tame* bird made a good pet. **tamer, tamest.**

ter·ri·ble (ter′ə bəl) *adjective.* awful; horrible: The *terrible* storm destroyed the road.

tide (tīd) *noun.* the rise and fall of the ocean twice a day caused by the pull of the sun and the moon: Let's go fishing at high *tide.*

tim·er (tī′mər) *noun.* a thing that keeps track of time: The *timer* went off when the meat was done.

to·ward (tôrd or tə wôrd′) *preposition.* 1. in the direction of: He walked *toward* the pond. 2. close to; near.

tow·el (tou′əl) *noun.* a piece of cloth used for drying or wiping: Marsha dried her hands on a *towel.*

towns·peo·ple (touns′pē′pəl) *noun.* people who live in a particular area or town.

traf·fic (traf′ik) *noun.* people, wagons, or cars coming and going on a roadway: The police were called in to control the heavy *traffic.*

trav·el (trav′əl) *verb.* 1. to go from one place to another: Some people *travel* by train. 2. move. **traveled, traveling.**

Tues·day (tüz′dē or tyüz′dē) *noun.* third day of the week, coming between Monday and Wednesday.

tun·nel (tun′l) *noun.* a passage underground: The *tunnel* goes under the city.

twin·kle (twing′kəl) *verb.* to sparkle: His eyes *twinkled* with delight. **twinkled, twinkling.**

U

un·der·stand (un′dər stand′) *verb.* 1. to know well: Mother usually *understands* me. 2. to get the meaning of.

u·ni·form (yü′nə fôrm) *noun.* clothes that are alike worn by members of a group: The band *uniforms* were blue and white. —*adjective.* not changing; the same.

un·spo·ken (un spō′kən) *adjective.* not said: There are many *unspoken* ways to communicate.

un·u·su·al (un yü′zhü əl) *adjective.* different; rare; uncommon.

W

Wash·ing·ton (wosh′ing tən or wô′shing tən) *noun.* 1. capital of the United States of America. 2. one of the states of the United States. 3. (George Washington) first president of the United States.

wheat (hwēt) *noun.* a grain that is ground into flour for making bread.

wheel·bar·row (hwēl′bar′ō) *noun.* a cart of wood or metal having one wheel in front and two long handles in back; used for moving heavy loads.

win (win) *verb.* to finish first; to beat others. **won, winning.**

Win·nie-the-Pooh (win′ē ᖘHə pü′) *noun.* an animal character in stories by A. A. Milne.

wom·en (wim′ən) *noun.* (plural) more than one woman.

won (wun) *verb.* finished first. *See* **win.**

world (wėrld) *noun.* 1. all people; the public. 2. earth.

wor·thy (wėr′ᖘHē) *adjective.* 1. deserving praise: Helping people is a *worthy* cause. 2. having value. **worthier, worthiest.**

Y

yeast (yēst) *noun.* the substance that makes bread dough rise.

(*Acknowledgments continued from page 2*)

by permission of Dodd, Mead & Company, Inc. from *The Lonely Dancer and Other Poems* by Richard LeGallienne. Copyright 1913 by Dodd, Mead & Company, Inc. Copyright renewed 1941 by Richard LeGalliene.

Editions Gallimard, Paris, for "Crafty Cardboard Houses," adapted from *Games for a Rainy Day* by Maurice Pipard. Used by permission.

Gakken Co., Ltd., for "The Fox and the Stork," adapted from "The Fox and the Crane" in *Aesop's Fables*. Courtesy Gakken Co., Ltd., Tokyo, Japan.

Ginn and Company for "Watching Animals" on page 69, from *Elementary Science 3* by Jeanne Bendick and Roy A. Gallant, © Copyright, 1980, by Ginn and Company (Xerox Corporation). Also for "City Government" on page 171, from *Our Communities* by Eleanor Thomas and Sara Beattie with Ernest W. Tiegs and Fay Adams of *Our Land and Heritage* series, © Copyright, 1979, by Ginn and Company (Xerox Corporation). Both used by permission of the publisher.

Hastings House, Publishers, Inc., for "About Dogs," adapted from *Seven True Dog Stories* by Margaret Davidson, Copyright © '77, permission by Hastings House, Publishers.

Highlights for Children for "A Special Pocket" by Jane F. Benoist, adapted from *Highlights for Children*, November 1978. Copyright © 1978, Highlights for Children, Inc., Columbus, Ohio. Used by permission.

Edmund Lindop for "The First Balloon Flight in North America," adapted from his book *George Washington and the First Balloon Flight*. Published by Albert Whitman & Company, Chicago. Used by permission of the author.

Margaret Moore and John Travers Moore for "The Little Band," adapted and abridged from their book *The Little Band and the Inaugural Parade* copyright 1968 by Margaret Moore and John Travers Moore and published by Albert Whitman & Co. Used by permission of the authors.

Penguin Books Ltd, London, for "Flashlight" from pages 8-9 of *Flashlight and Other Poems* by Judith Thurman. (Kestrel, 1977) Reprinted by permission of Penguin Books Ltd.

The Society of Authors, London, for the poem "I Meant to Do My Work Today" by Richard LeGallienne from his book *The Lonely Dancer*. Reprinted by permission of The Society of Authors as the literary representative of the Estate of Richard LeGallienne.

Illustrators and Photographers: Peter Bradford, cover, 8-9, 84-85, 154-155, 222-223; William McDade, 1, 3-7, 40-41, 48-49, 68-69, 82-83, 100-101, 120-121, 130-131, 152-153, 170-171, 188-189, 206-207, 220-221, 236-237, 254-255, 262-263, 284-285, 306-317; Kevin Young, 8-9, 84-85, 154-155, 222-223; Seymour Chwast, 10-19, 138-151, 224-231; Michael L. Pateman, 20-23, 42-47, 256-261; Tomie DePaola, 24-39; Paul M. Gleason, 50-59; Don Weller, 60-65, 77-81; David Cain, 66-67; Carol Inouye, 70-76; Jenny Rutherford, 86-95; Carolyn McHenry, 96-99, 111-119, 190-199; Gary Kelley, 102-110, 122-129; Cliff Condak, 132-137; Roseanne Litzinger, 156-169; Diane deGroat, 182-185; Kristen Dietrich, 186-187; Sandy Rabinowitz, 200-205; A. A. Milne, 208-219; Barbara Morgan, 232-235; Cathy Bennett, 238-253; Stephen Ogilvy, 264-266; Kyoshi Kanai, 267-271; Terry Presnall, 272-283; Tommy Soloski, 286-305.

Design, Ginn Reading Program:
Creative Director: Peter Bradford
Art Director: Gary Fujiwara
Design Coordinator: Anne Todd
Design: Lorraine Johnson, Linda Post, Kevin Young, Cathy Bennett, Kristen Dietrich

CDEFGHIJO876543
Printed in the United States of America